BLACK SUCCESS

THE SURPRISING TRUTH

Tony Sewell

FORUM

FORUM

First published in Great Britain by Forum, an imprint of Swift Press 2024

1 3 5 7 9 8 6 4 2

Copyright © Tony Sewell 2024

The right of Tony Sewell to be identified as the Author of this Work has been asserted in accordance with the Copyright, Designs and Patents Act 1988.

Printed and bound in Great Britain by CPI

A CIP catalogue record for this book is available from the British Library

ISBN: 9781800752269
eISBN: 9781800752276

CONTENTS

CONTENTS

Our crown has already been bought and paid for.
All we have to do is wear it.

JAMES BALDWIN

Walk like a champion.

BUJU BANTON

I feel the same about the Black Lives Matter
movement, its very name a sort of bleat. Give me
Black Power, every time.

MATTHEW PARRIS

Men at some time are masters of their fates:
The fault, dear Brutus, is not in our stars,
But in ourselves, that we are underlings.

WILLIAM SHAKESPEARE

We run tings, tings nuh run we.

FLOURGON

ACKNOWLEDGEMENTS

I am happy to say that this work was inspired by several great souls. I need to thank Kathy Watson, who has been a wonderful guide throughout, making sure that wisdom prevailed over vanity. A special thanks must go to my publisher, George Owers, for having the faith and helping me through various drafts. Likewise to my agent Matthew Hamilton, who has been with me from the beginning. Particular thanks must go to Adele and Zindzi, who knew that after the storm would come the calm. And a special dedication to my old professor, the late Dudley Young, who continues to be in the wind and the trees.

Lastly I owe thanks to all those at Sewellness Park, Jamaica who worked hard while I was writing – save me some mangoes.

INTRODUCTION

FROM BRIXTON
TO THE HOUSE OF LORDS

F OR black people of my generation, those three days and nights in April 1981 are defining. The Brixton Riots were nothing less than a black youth rebellion.

From the beginning of the month, the police had been using (and abusing) laws allowing them to stop and search people if they suspected wrongdoing. In so-called 'Operation Swamp', they focussed on areas with large numbers of black residents. Places like Brixton. There was an obvious point of friction between black unemployed youths and a police force that deliberately targeted them using the full force of the law.

At the time, I was in London – back from Essex University, where I was in my third year of a degree in English Literature. On the morning of Sunday 12 April, my brother and I were in church in Penge. Penge is just a few miles south of Brixton, but that day it felt like it belonged to a parallel universe. Our church had a predominantly white congregation. The riots were ongoing and, both at church and on the streets, people looked at me as though I were one of the rioters.

This was the biggest social justice issue of the day. But my church had no comment to make. As the sermon rang in my ears, I felt conflicted. Jesus, surely, would have been at the front of the crowds just a couple of miles down the road, screaming for fairness. He wouldn't be here, praying for a better world from the safe cloisters of a church in Penge. He would be out there, making it happen.

After the service, my brother and I left the church both physically and emotionally, as we took the 20-minute bus ride to Brixton. The details of that weekend are well documented: injuries to police and civilians; buildings damaged; vehicles torched. The pictures are still terrifying: rows of police with riot shields, upturned cars, burning buildings, crowds of angry, frightened people.

That night, we met a policeman from Yorkshire. The Met had been bringing in police from all over the UK. He was in Brixton, and he was hopelessly lost.

'Do you know how to get to Railton Road?' he asked, in a thick Yorkshire burr. Of course I did. Railton Road, scene of the most violent clashes, was just a stone's throw from my birth-place. Our exchange summed up the madness for me. People like this officer, probably well-meaning enough in their own way, were being brought in from distant parts of the country to police places and communities they had no understanding of.

When the dust settled, Lord Scarman was commissioned by the Conservative government to investigate the causes of the uprising, and race disparities in the UK more generally. His report was published in November 1981, and it can be seen as the first attempt to understand some of the issues facing the children of the Windrush Generation.

Out of the ashes of the riots came reporting of another kind, a different attempt to understand and sort through these issues: *The Voice* newspaper. This publication gave the descendants of the post-war generation an opportunity to speak about all the things that mattered to them most: love, humour, music, politics and money. Speaking to and for British-born African-Caribbean people, *The Voice* became one of the most successful black businesses in Britain, and one of the clearest examples of disadvantage being turned into advantage. I worked for the paper as a reporter, arts editor, commissioned historian and columnist spanning 15 years. Many top journalists have said to me that I was lucky to have such an exciting apprenticeship.

This book – and maybe my whole adult life – has been part of the process of exorcising the ghosts of 1981. We should never forget the terrible injustices; but at the same time, we need to clear a mental pathway for a new generation. We should avoid Pollyannaism, but we need to tell a new, positive story about ourselves. We need to be alive to injustice but celebrate our successes. All this requires skilful mental juggling. We must acknowledge the suffering of our parents and grandparents, but not be burdened with their trauma. Rather, inspired by their example of resilience and fortitude, we must create our own drive and agency in order to move forward.

The Voice is a perfect example of what I'm talking about. Out of the fires of the riots came a successful, forward-looking business. Despite the constant background hum of disadvantage, entrepreneurial people spotted an opportunity. When our mindset is driven by the great power of individual agency, by belief in our own abilities, we can achieve anything. This is what black success looks like. And here's the surprising truth: it's already happening.

*

In May 2020, George Floyd, a 46-year-old African-American man, was killed in Minneapolis. Police officer Derek Chauvin was later convicted of his murder. The video showing Floyd under the knee of a white policeman went across the world. In Britain, we staged copycat protests to the ones in America. Many of these protests were organised by Black Lives Matter and Stand Up to Racism. They quickly moved from the streets to companies, charities, local government and celebrities, all bending the knee in solidarity. All this happened amidst the first wave of Covid and the unprecedented UK lockdown.

When the dust settled, the then Conservative government commissioned me to write a report about race disparities in Britain. That report was published on 31 March 2021.

Two sets of disorders, two government reports, 40 years apart. There are enough similarities to make this the perfect moment to stop and reflect. What has changed? What real progress has been made since 1981? What are the differences between then and now?

There are some differences that I feel have been overlooked.

The Brixton disorders in 1981 were explicitly rooted in injustice in the UK. They were given international coverage, but nonetheless it was a local fight, arising out of distinctly British issues. The young people were predominantly African-Caribbean, the UK's majority black population at the time. The protestors tended to be poor. They suffered from a lack of qualifications and high unemployment. The focus of their rebellion was heavy-handed police tactics.

The protests in 2020 were different. There were more white protesters, more students, more graduates, more profession-als, more professional activists. Many of the young black people involved were not disaffected youth – unemployed, impoverished, pulled over by police time and time again. This cohort were at university or college, and they were protesting against 'white privilege' as well as police brutality. Anger was directed towards statues of nineteenth-century slave owners, names of school buildings, and the casting decisions of Hollywood movies. There weren't specific laws or policies that protesters were seeking to reform – beyond changes to the KS3 curriculum.

The demonstrations were seen by some as a second, and long overdue, black awakening. During one demonstration, I saw a young black man dancing beautifully up the steps of St Martin-in-the-Fields in central London. The crowd was roaring him on as the loudspeakers played Diana Ross's wonderful success anthem 'I'm Coming Up'. To me, it summed up some of the complexity of that demonstration, and showed it was a world away from the uprisings of 1981. Did this protest of 'black power', inspired by events abroad, mean a new level of black militancy had taken over a new generation? No, this young man was more likely to be at university, heading to a great degree and a top job in the City. The numbers show that he was more likely to go into higher education than any low-income white youth in the north of England.

Some 40 years earlier, the Scarman Report had identified the Brixton disorders as a spontaneous eruption fuelled by a combination of general resentment and some specific incidents. Scarman placed them within a context of 'complex political, social and economic factors'. He noted the problems of racial disadvantage and inner-city decline. Action was needed, and that action needed to be 'urgent'. According to his report, 'institutional racism' did not exist, but there needed to be a policy of 'direct coordinated attack on racial disadvantage'.

What made 2020 different? Instead of a recession, we had lockdown. Police actions triggered the protests, but those actions took place on the other side of the world. It wasn't always clear how the American inciting incident fitted into the British context. Sometimes it felt as if we had borrowed another country's racial tensions and added them to our own.

I was asked by the government to use this opportunity to have a serious conversation about race disparities in Britain. The rhetoric of the British protests needed to be tested against the facts and the data. What was the real situation of the black community? I became the chair of a new Commission on Race and Ethnic Disparities. The remit was straightforward: to review racial disparities focussing on areas such as poverty, education, employment, health and the criminal justice system.

After a long period of research, we offered our findings. The Report made two particularly important observations:

- That there are indeed disparities for many groups relating to education, employment, crime and health – but that the majority of these did not originate from racism.
- That racism does still exist: the Report found that there are historic issues of trust, which remain real and important – but that things are improving, particularly in education and employment.

The Report was received by some as an attempt to deny the reality of institutional racism. There followed what felt like a campaign to discredit our work and undermine its findings. However, there were also many who could see that this was a radical report with common-sense findings, and the government began to put into place many of the recommendations.

Because they made sense. For example, the UK soon established its first Office for Health Disparities, which tackles issues such as high mortality rates for black women in childbirth.

The Report found many examples of black success. For example, in 2019 the average GCSE attainment score of eight for black African pupils was above that of white British pupils. 66.9% of black African young people had progressed to higher education by the age of 19. In key health outcomes, including life expectancy, overall mortality and many leading causes of death, ethnic minority groups have better outcomes than the white population. People with African-Caribbean heritage are more likely to own their own homes than other ethnic minority groups. Black women have better employment rates than their white counterparts and the ethnicity pay gap is decreasing (in 2019 it was 2.3% – down from 8.2% in 2015). Among the under-30s who are employed, there are no significant pay gaps for any ethnic minority group.

It's not a bad tally at all, especially for a group that has only lived in the UK in significant numbers since the 1950s. Yet, the prevailing narrative is one of riots, gloom and despair – interspersed with flashes of sporting or musical genius. In the popular consciousness, black people seem to live at one of two poles – an inner-city world of failure, violence and criminality, or the red-carpet world of celebrities, excellence and awards.

In this book I want to tell other stories, about other kinds of excellence. The quiet everyday success of living a healthy life and buying property, of doing well at school and raising a family. The triumphs of independence and agency – of the individual and the entrepreneur.

In these success stories, I thought I might find not just a balance to the negative stories, but also a roadmap for the black community as a whole. Indeed, these stories provide a template that could be used by anyone, irrespective of their background and ethnicity.

Currently, there is a culture – often coming from well-meaning, but potentially patronising white people – that says black people have no control and no agency over their own experiences. It says that they are fixed in a system that is inevitably and always hostile to them.

I think that is wrong.

You can, and must, point to exceptions to the positive trend. For instance, the 'hostile environment' deliberately created by ex-prime minster Theresa May's immigration policies. The hostile environment resulted in a number of longstanding residents being deported or unable to participate fully in our society. This was wrong, a clear injustice. The government was right to compensate the victims. However, even in this case the vast majority regularised their status once they were aware of the change in the law. The British government should have been more aware of how this would impact those in Caribbean communities. Still, it would have been useful to hear also from those who did manage to change their status. There is a risk that the Windrush scandal has made the black community out to be helpless and hapless – people with no agency in the world around them.

*

I am writing this book in the same year that the iconic black actor Sydney Poitier died, at the age of 94. Poitier was a man who rarely lost his cool, but in 1968 he finally snapped:

You could ask me many questions about many positive and wonderful things that are happening in this country, but we gather here to pay court to sensationalism. We gather here to pay court to negativism ... you ask me one-dimensional questions that fall continually within the 'negro-ness' of my life. I am artist, man, American, contemporary, I am an awful lot of things, so I wish you would pay me the respect due and not simply ask me about those things.

Poitier points to a key plank in my theory of black success. It is about not allowing race to dominate your humanity.

This is also the view taken by the educator Ian Rowe, who like me comes from Jamaican stock but in his case made a mark in America. In some ways Ian's career has a wonderful resemblance to my own. When he told me that my Report and my interviews had changed his life, I felt flattered that Tony Sewell, a poor boy from Brixton, could have an impact on one of the big thinkers in America.

Rowe is six years younger than me, and in the 1960s his parents, like mine, migrated from Jamaica – in their case to Brooklyn, New York City. My parents had made a similar journey when they took the plane to London in the 1950s. According to Ian, the family 'moved up' and ultimately settled in Laurelton, a white middle-class neighbourhood. We likewise graduated from Brixton to a mixed but predominantly white area called Penge. Like Laurelton, Penge would see an increase in its black population but never really suffered the major racial tensions that marred Ian's American suburb. His high school, like mine, closed down after it was marked as one of the worst in the district.

Ian's parents didn't go straight to America. As his father, Vincent, wanted to pursue a degree in engineering, he travelled first to England, where he was able to work on the buses and study part-time. He sent for his love, Eula, who came to Britain to work as a nurse in 1955. And seven years later Ian was born, so technically he is a Londoner. According to Ian, the next adventure was to go to the United States, where his dad got a job at IBM and his mum worked as an analyst with the Manufacturers Hanover Bank. At this point in his story, it struck me that Ian was on his way to becoming part of the Jamaican middle class in America; by contrast, in 1960s Britain most Jamaicans were stuck in the low-income class and only a minority were able to move up. I always wondered how Ian would have progressed if his parents hadn't moved to America. I am convinced that, like me, he would have taken advantage of the biggest opportunity on offer and got himself a free university education. Of course, with the introduction of student fees in 1998, things have changed from those good old days.

The story of Ian's parents also helps to demystify some of the tropes around the Windrush legacy. They were not enticed by some noble calling to the mother country, any more than my own parents had been. They were simply running towards better economic conditions and away from the boredom of the Jamaican countryside. Money and adventure. They were not conned, they just took a risk; and in their case, as in that of my parents, it paid out for them and their children.

Like me, Ian benefitted from three pillars of security that helped him forge his way to success. The first was his family and the extended Jamaican family in New York; the second was his church and Christian upbringing; and the third was an innate passion to make his own way and not allow any negativity to thwart his goals. Ian calls this third factor 'Agency' and sees it as having two main characteristics: 'agility' and an underlying vision or agenda.

For Ian, as for me, the big exam question was not the fight for freedom but *how* to be free. The three pillars provide an answer to the question and a framework for living, one that Ian calls FREE – an acronym for Family, Religion, Education and Enterprise.

During the aftermath of the publication of my Report, I was the subject of an excellent interview in the *Wall Street Journal*. Ian read the story and was moved to get in touch. This is how, in a recent email, he recalls the influence of that article:

> The first time I encountered Tony Sewell was in the pages of the *Wall Street Journal*. Here was a fellow black Jamaican in his adopted homeland – in Sewell's case Great Britain, in mine the United States of America – engaged in a similar struggle to make sense of his country's racial disparities, working to determine the best path forward to drive upward mobility.
>
> America was in the midst of a national reckoning on race in the aftermath of the death of George Floyd, triggering Britain to embark upon a racial journey of its own. In 'The Report That Shook Britain's Race Lobby', Sewell shared with the *WSJ* his experience as the Chairman of Britain's Commission on Race and Ethnic Disparities. The expectation was that the commission would invoke the usual suspects of white privilege and systemic bias to be the all-purpose explanations for any instance of racial inequality.
>
> Instead, the report 'concluded that while Britain isn't yet "a post-racial society", neither is it any longer a place where "the system" is "deliberately rigged against ethnic minorities"'.

Sewell and his 10-member commission, almost all of whom were ethnic minorities, offered a different hypothesis: 'In many areas of investigation, including educational failure and crime, we were led upstream to family breakdown as one of the main reasons for poor outcomes. Family is also the foundation stone of success for many ethnic minorities.'

I felt I had met in Sewell a kindred spirit. As a Senior Fellow at the American Enterprise Institute, I researched the force that was typically at the heart of the perpetual cycle of economic disadvantage that has plagued certain communities. And in my own experience leading public charter schools in low-income communities in the Bronx, I had come to a similar realization: Family structure, and in particular the prevalence of single-parent homes, was a far more predictive factor driving poverty.

In time, I had the pleasure of meeting Sewell, and invited him to participate in a discussion on black advancement drawing on [Thomas Sowell's book] *The Economics and Politics of Race*. Ultimately, I quoted Sewell in my own book *Agency*: 'As our investigations proceeded, we increasingly felt that an unexplored approach to closing disparity gaps was to examine the extent individuals and their communities could help themselves through their own agency, rather than wait for invisible external forces to assemble to do the job.'

In 2021 I received an email from America asking me to contribute to what turned out to be a wonderful conference in Texas. Glenn Loury and Shelby Steele were heading the ticket and I proudly played for England. So many of the audience had already read and loved my Report that I felt like one of those black British actors getting a leading film role.

Not only did the conference go well, but Ian Rowe invited me to his own conference in Salt Lake City, Utah. It was here that we were able to perform a double act, sharing our rich Jamaican roots and preaching the new gospel of Agency. The American audience were intrigued to hear two black men from different continents preaching a similar message about family, enterprise, education and religion. Where our stars are truly aligned is that we both ended up running top education programmes for young people in the inner cities. Ian managed to run one of the best Charter school programmes in America, and I have delivered great outcomes with our STEM Generating Genius programme in Britain. We are now planning a joint US and UK speaking tour, where we hope to inspire a generation about the real power of Agency.

Derek Walcott, the Nobel prize-winning St Lucian poet, was one of the best chroniclers of the Caribbean, colonialism and the role of memory. His essay 'Café Martinique' is an examination of how the past holds on to us and holds us back. At the end of the essay, he writes, 'The century has turned.' To those who can't let go of the past, he says, 'It is you who are waiting. And only you know what for. Meanwhile the rest of us have things to do. We move ahead.'

*

How did Britain's 1950s Caribbean settlers find a route to prosperity? Why are Nigerians achieving so highly in the education system? Why do Jamaicans run so fast? How is Britain producing a conveyor belt of young black scientists?

So much of what we think we know about 'black communities' is rooted in misery and victimhood. This is not to diminish the reality of racism, but as Jamaican singer Dennis Brown would say, 'What about the half that has never been told?' This book tells that half.

Who is it for? People who are fair-minded. People who haven't got a political axe to grind, who are open to listening to facts and examining the data. People who would like to hear a different story from the usual one about endless racism and relentless discrimination. People who would like to see which other more optimistic stories might exist and how they might shape their own lives in a positive direction. I hope, most of all, that people will read this book and feel inspired.

The book is divided into two parts. In the first we will look at my experiences in the education sector, and my own experiences of education and work, to see what are the ingredients that determine black success. I'll walk you through a roughly chronological version of my life, taking in my own schooling, my time as a columnist and academic, and my experiences taking over a failing education system in East London and running an education charity for gifted black boys in STEM.

In the second half of the book, we look at examples of black success in surprising places. We're going to celebrate that success and ask why examples of success in the mainstream – for instance in home ownership and entrepreneurship – are often overlooked, or tweaked to make a different story. To move ahead, there are things that black people must do. We must take hold of the fact that society is more open than it was in the past, especially in terms of legalities. We must believe that our actions can influence our outcomes. There are opportunities out there and we must take hold of them. That might mean going outside our own community, to the places where we imagine we don't belong. This might be uncomfortable. But a degree of discomfort is an essential ingredient to success. As are education and training. Bringing things full circle, we'll examine some of the ways in which black people, especially the children of African immigrants, have excelled in the education system. We'll also look at class. Low-income white people have a lot in common with their black peers. Identity politics has got in the way of finding this potentially progressive common ground.

We need, then, to enjoy the successes of black people and, where possible, to describe and reproduce their steps so more black people can succeed. If readers take away the belief that, through their own effort and imagination, they can change their circumstances and their world while still holding onto a sense of social justice, I will be happy.

For that to happen, we must let go of the narrative that our fate is fixed by a hostile society. I want to see if there can be a way of acknowledging the injustices of the past while leaving them in the past, so that they are not allowed to blight our presents and our futures. Many battles have been fought and won. Black people suffered in the past – on the Middle Passage, in Caribbean plantations, in a hostile Britain – and yet many people broke through and escaped, fought back and challenged discrimination. It's not that we should ignore past atrocities, but we don't have to be paralysed by them.

The quote that guides this book comes from James Baldwin. It was also used by Maya Angelou. 'Your crown has been bought and paid for. Put it on your head and wear it.'

PART 1

EDUCATION

I

PENGE

THE SCHOOL OF HARD KNOCKS

I WENT to a bog-standard secondary modern school in the 1970s – which is to say a failing school. Most of us graduated in 'football and fighting'.

I had to get my classical education in alternative spaces. I point to four: my local library, where I worked part-time as a librarian; reggae music; Clive Lloyd's West Indian cricket team; and my local Church of England Sunday school.

This education occurred against a backdrop of open racism, which for me mostly took the form of name-calling on the streets. It was reinforced by blatant and constant police harassment. Many of my generation were traumatised by this experience. Many have never, and will never, recover.

But, for myself, this early bout of racism didn't traumatise me, slow my development or dent my confidence. Why? Some would say I was lucky, others that I was just thick-skinned. I don't think it's either. The real saviour was Sunday school and those instructive stories from the Good Book. They took me away from race and reminded me of my greater humanity.

My Sunday school was predominantly white and middle class. Through the church, I entered a world that was more aspirational than the one I was familiar with at my failing school. Yes, my fellow Christians were guilty of ignoring the wider racism in society, but I didn't need their empathy. I only needed my fellow churchgoers to be themselves – to be fair, decent and loving. It was a wonderful escape from the madness around us.

Sunday school was my early university. Along with Greek mythology, it gave me a good grasp of the classics. For me, there was never a gap between a so-called Eurocentric grounding and an Afrocentric one. What I experienced was a wonderful synergy: I had white Sunday school coupled with the Jamaican reggae revival of the 1970s. Here too I found Judaeo-Christian stories and beliefs. On Sunday morning, I would learn the story of the children of Israel making their Exodus from Babylon – then go home to jump up to a reggae version of the same story. The songs of Bob Marley and Desmond Dekker meant that we had great theology and great pop music blaring out of the West Indian front room.

I saw myself as culturally privileged and felt very sorry for the white children in my school. They never went to church, and they were deeply envious of the new Jamaican popular culture that was sweeping London. I literally had the best of both worlds.

Although this story is personal, I think a lot of people will identify with it. I'm sure plenty of people will nod along in agreement when I say that there are, ironically, advantages to coming from a place that seems to have few or no advantages. We've been told a particular story about these things and I want to tell another one – starting with my own.

STRAIGHT OUTTA PENGE

Penge is a south-east London suburb. It sits within the London Borough of Bromley and is located 7.1 miles south-east of Charing Cross.

The Rolling Stones' Bill Wyman went to the local grammar, Kentwood School, and his band was supposedly formed above the sweet shop opposite. David Bowie, born in neighbouring Beckenham, wrote the lyric, 'It's a very special knowledge that you've got my friend; you can walk around in New York while you sleep in Penge.'

For Bowie, Penge was a place you disengaged from. I lived there for more than a decade. I was born in Brixton, the spiritual headquarters of the black British community; it was there that many Caribbean migrants settled from the 1950s onwards. But my mother wanted to break away from the inner city and looked to the sunny uplands of sleepy Penge. So, we moved there when I was about four, and I stayed until I went to university.

Penge was contradictory. It had a mainly poor, majority white population at the time; yet when it came to elections, we always sent back a Conservative MP. That was because the borough was conjoined with our richer and bigger neighbour, Beckenham, whose residents would never dream of voting Labour.

For my inner-city cousins in Brixton or other black enclaves such as Hackney, Tottenham or Harlesden, Penge was 'the countryside'. Why would anyone live out there, especially if you were black? They had a point. In the 1960s and 1970s, overt racism was wide and bold. Outside of the inner city, we had our share, mainly the constant shouting of the n-word by people driving by. This happened most intensely when I was at primary school. The issue of open racial abuse in the 1970s was tough – not only for me, but for my parents, who couldn't really protect us from it. It wasn't just National Front hooligan types. It also came from older people, who would sneeringly tell us: 'Go back to your own country'. The idea of being black and British seemed to pose a problem for many people. Asked 'Where do you come from?', many of us got tired of the continued interrogation if we said London or Penge, so simply said Kingston, Jamaica, even though we had never been there. But as time wore on, Penge improved. Eventually, we found it to be a warm community, full of characters.

Our only contact with our grandparents came in the form (pre-internet) of blue airmail letters from Jamaica. The writers were my maternal grandmother and my paternal grandfather. We would rush downstairs to grab the letters and look in amazement at their beautiful handwriting and flawless grammar. We, on the other hand, were stuck in the so-called mother country barely literate after years in London state schools. The idea of being constrained by a 'white curriculum' and needing to go on a journey of black enlightenment to escape the influence of dead white men would have seemed ridiculous to me – I wanted an education like my grandparents.

I went to secondary school in the 1970s, the age of flared trousers, the three-day week, paraffin heaters and the 11-plus exam. Undoubtedly, the last of these had the greatest effect on society and on me. To understand my history, you need a quick tour of this wonderful British institution. In many ways, it's as strange as the history of our monarchy. It was also a great commodity that Britain exported to its former colonies, many of whom still cling to it with a passion.

The exam was introduced in 1944, when, under the Butler Education Act, the schooling system in the UK was rearranged. All children aged between five and ten attended primary schools, and then, at the age of 11, they took an exam: depending on whether they passed or failed, they then went to an academic grammar school or to a secondary modern or technical institution.

Many politicians felt that the 11-plus system was unfair on less academically minded children. What seems clear in retrospect is that the move towards a comprehensive system was always based on a drive towards equality rather than educational considerations.

In many ways, the 11-plus exam represented the hidden beast of England – our class system, in which everyone was supposed to know their place. As we would sing in assembly, in the now redacted lines of 'All things bright and beautiful':

> The rich man in his castle, the poor man at his gate,
> God made them, high or lowly, and ordered their estate.

I failed the 11-plus and ended up in a secondary modern. Halfway through my time there, it became a comprehensive school.

Looking back, I still feel sorry for the new first-years at my school, standing around awkwardly in their neatly pressed uniforms as they were targeted by the thugs in the fourth form. One particular image stands out in memory: a tiny 11-year-old standing alone in the distant playing field and this small dot being eaten up by a stampede of about a hundred boys. When they had finished, they left a forlorn figure barely able to stand, uniform in shreds, his bags and books strewn across the field.

When I saw that, I was determined to escape. But how? Most young people left school at 16 and went straight to work. If you were black, you went to the local college to do City and Guilds courses. University was a place for the middle class.

The superhead of TV's *Educating Essex*, Vic Goddard, who was brought up in Penge and went to my school, says in his book, 'I was very lucky because the school was tough; all boys, culturally diverse, testosterone-laden and lots of them bussed out to the 'burbs from inner London.'

This idea of it being 'lucky' to attend a failing school is an interesting comment. But I know what Goddard means. Toughness made us. We were the first guinea pigs of the new comprehensive system and we had to fight to get out of the cage. The school gave Vic Goddard the drive and empathy he needed to be a great headteacher. It inspired me to be part of a future movement that would radically change the comprehensive school system forever. Disadvantage was turned to advantage and that became personal and social change.

The little boy caught up in that stampede had a rude awakening. He may have had some apprehension about his new school, but he couldn't have expected that kind of battering. And although Kentwood did have people like Vic and myself who succeeded, a lot of students failed and ended up going nowhere, their dreams and ambitions scattered around them. The new comprehensive system couldn't carry the majority across the line. The schools were no better than the secondary moderns they were set up to replace.

When I first went to Kentwood, I felt cheated by the unfairness of the 11-plus system that had dumped me into a substandard secondary school. However, it is interesting to look back at this period using our current lens. Today, people talk about 'white privilege'. My school was two-thirds white and a third African-Caribbean. Comprehensive education didn't discriminate: the schools gave an equally terrible education to all.

There was, however, one obvious disparity that was clearly an example of structural racism. At my school, when you asked most of the white boys where they were going to work, they either talked about some sort of building trade with their uncle, or getting a job at the *Daily Mirror*, in the print department. The unions had full control, not just of wages and conditions, but also over who was hired. They ran a corrupt network that ensured that the sons of the print-workers were next in line for new jobs. One of the practices that worked against black applicants was the reliance of companies on word-of-mouth recruitment, as opposed to advertising or using the careers service.

Margaret Thatcher was elected with a mandate to 'tame the unions' after Labour's Winter of Discontent in 1978–79. Britain had become a miserable place with endless strikes, rubbish on the streets, and a general sense of doom and gloom. London in particular was in need of a makeover. Thatcher implemented new labour laws that outlawed closed shops and secondary picketing and made secret ballots compulsory, instead of mass show-of-hands voting. It was Rupert Murdoch, the newspaper baron, who first used these new laws to break the unions' power base. This was most visible when he was able to cut his labour costs by using new computerised technology at his Wapping plant in East London. Thatcher cut nepotism from an organisation that was meant to stand for fairness and equality.

There were other barriers that blocked access to employment. The key one was skills. Following our terrible schooling, many of my generation lacked the skills to succeed in a modern economy. This continued into the next generation. Even though some white boys did have escape routes to employment, as mentioned, there was still an enormous class barrier in the 1970s and 1980s. Both black and white youth suffered from a poor education system and slim employment prospects.

So, with all these problems in mind, how did I, and many others like me, manage to live successful and happy lives? The reasons are complex and counter-intuitive; they suggest that conventional myths about black success need to be unpicked.

So, let's take a tour of Penge, and I'll offer a brief autobiography – to unpack the secrets of black success.

THE GOOD, THE BAD, AND THE LIBRARY

We start on the famous Maple Road. Back in the 1970s, most of our markets were uncovered. They were the source of all our fruit and vegetables. I remember Davis the florist, which must have supplied flowers for countless Penge weddings, birthdays and funerals. All the black people in Penge seemed to know each other, but the town generally had a feeling of togetherness. No one could pull any airs and graces: we were all low-income and it gave us a sense of solidarity.

My mother was one of the dons in Penge market. Everyone knew her. Shops and traders knew not to cross her. They called her by her first name and were worried when they didn't see her. At the top of the road, George the grocer had to have my mother's Uncle Ben's rice ready. The lady who sold the eggs looked after my mother's shopping trolley while she made her way to the butchers. The best cut of meat had better be ready for her, and there was always laughing and joking. Jamaicans say: 'We run tings, tings nuh run we', which translated means 'we are in charge of circumstances, we don't let circumstances control us.' Penge market was my first lesson in this kind of confidence-building. My mother was not going to be traumatised by the reality of the racism that existed in the UK. Like most of my parents' generation, she knew what needed to be done. Weekly trips to the market with my mother were a masterclass in control, confidence and agency.

My parents' generation often struggled to get bank loans because of discrimination. This forced the Caribbean community to invent their own credit service. My mother ran one of these informal banking schemes, which was called 'Pardners'. Pardners was a way in which you could raise a large sum of money, usually to purchase large, significant items such as furniture. My mum would collect everyone's money and, at the end of the week or month, one of the participants would get the total in a lump sum. The usual practice was that when your 'hand' came around, you would tip the banker. There had been scandals of bankers running off with the cash. However, like all great bankers, my mother had integrity and a grasp of the finer numerical details.

She worked in a small electronic components factory in Penge, about 800 metres from our house. My mother was the only black woman there, surrounded by about 50 white men. She loved it, saying that she preferred to work with men. I felt sorry for the men. They didn't dare forget her birthday and, if anyone messed with her workstation, there would be no mercy. My mother used her networking skills to get a number of black youths jobs in the factory: this was her way of balancing the nepotism that saw white boys getting jobs through their fathers' union connections. She was not naive about the reality of racism, but also had the confidence to use her own judgement and agency.

It was the same confidence, judgement, choice and agency that inspired her – and thousands like her – to leave the Caribbean and move abroad, some to America, some to Canada and some to the UK. They were inspired by a mixture of motives – adventure, ambition, curiosity – and they all made new and different lives for themselves.

Still, my mother wanted us to have a moral education similar to the one that she'd had in Jamaica. This would come from the supplementary education of Sunday schools. She had been sent to church and to Sunday school in Jamaica, and so would we in the UK. It was here that my mother's confidence seemed to have a fault line. Although they were happy to send their children, neither she nor my father ever came to church. Maybe this all-white setting was an integration project too far. Maybe they just wanted a lie-in on a Sunday morning.

So off we went, me and my brother and sister, to the local Anglican church. I was about eight. They made sure that we looked good: my sister with her neat yellow ribbons and my brother and I in our sharp suits. We were the only black people there, but still we went to the Sunday school each week and communion in the big church once a month.

As a child, my biggest anxieties all arose from my parents' flawed marriage. They would fight constantly and, underneath her confident exterior, my mother was profoundly depressed. I would often find myself stranded between my parents as they argued, usually about money or my father's inability to find meaningful work.

The church was an oasis of peace, a refuge from these problems. It was also a sanctuary from my school, which did not provide enough stimulus. As I grew up, I realised that the mainly middle-class white children I met in church all intended to go to university. Sunday school gave me an alternative vision for my future, and a set of more aspirational peers. I wanted to follow their path, not the one mapped out for me at Kentwood School. Sunday school, Cubs and Scouts and Christianity also provided what I call the 'law lines'. Having these rules in place helped me not to go off the rails. My story is not the conventional one of a white institution like the Church of England making me feel unwanted. It was quite the opposite. The people at church in Penge were supportive, caring and – most importantly – gave me a great education.

Going to my Sunday school was like going to a theological seminary. At 14, we were having deep discussions on predestination and grace. I was taken to top Bible conferences, always intellectually demanding. I had to borrow books and read regularly so I could keep up in the midweek Bible study. I also got the chance to travel outside of Penge. I would go on holiday with the families of the church elders. We went to Cornwall and the Lake District. The church opened my eyes, my mind, and my world.

There was another part of my environment that had a profound effect on any later successes I had. In the 1970s and 1980s, most young people over 16 had part-time jobs. The army of young European workers had not yet arrived. I had some fantastic holiday jobs during my college and university years. However, my generation never needed part-time jobs during term time because our grants were so generous, particularly if you were poor. Before university, I had a prized Saturday and holiday job in my local library. I'd always been a keen visitor to the library and got on with the head librarian. When a vacancy came up, he invited me for an interview. There were many applicants for the job, including the children of current librarians. I was the only black candidate. Still, I knew the library inside out and I got the job. I started work the next day. As a librarian, I was delighted to discover there was no limit to the number of books I could borrow. They also had a great collection of European classical music and jazz. Taken all in, my summer job opened my mind to ever more books, and my ears to a range of music that went far beyond what was played on the radio. Soon, I became an expert on Bach, Mozart and John Coltrane. And I had a few quid in my back pocket. What a deal!

I was the only black person doing English Literature in my year at university. But I think I stood out most because my theological grounding helped me to excel. The church had given me the foundational knowledge that I needed to understand the history of literature. We started with Milton's *Paradise Lost*, and I was on home territory here, because the Bible provides the mythic framework for this work. As for the academic environment, I had been attending conferences and lectures with my church group since the age of 14. I would always go up to my teachers at university and talk to them after the class, berating them for things I felt they'd missed and enthusing on the things I felt passionately about. They loved my interest. Soon, we were discussing the role of knowledge in *Hamlet* at Sunday dinner. I must have been the only student who was invited back to my lecturers' homes. I didn't have imposter syndrome; in fact, I imposed myself on them – and I loved it. After university, some of the lecturers became long-term friends.

When people ask me why I think the classics are so important, I point them to the great Caribbean thinker and writer

C. L. R. James. I see many parallels in my experience to his. Don't get me wrong, I'm not in his intellectual league – but we share a similar passion. James was a scholar of Greek and Latin, his first love was Shakespeare, and he adored the works of Thackeray. His most recent biographer, John L. Williams, is often baffled at how this anti-colonialist figure had such a great love for Western culture:

> There's the contradiction that would both trouble and inspire CLR for the rest of his life. He would always at once be both fierce critic and committed devotee of Western culture as refracted through the public-school code. It's a mix that is not exclusively, but is definitely very strongly, Trinidadian.[1]

I would say that this is true of the whole of the English-speaking Caribbean. The biographer ends his book by saying that James would have had great empathy with the Black Lives Matter movement. On one point, certainly, I beg to differ. He wouldn't understand the passion to decolonise the curriculum. What he would have advocated is teaching young minds about that wonderful and painful 'contradiction' which is the Caribbean experience. He knew it was a privilege to be able to keep the baby while throwing out the bath water.

As for me, I realised very early that the remaking of Caribbean culture would always bear the influence of our European and African heritage. James was not prepared to slay those cultural influences that enhanced his humanity, like Shakespeare or Homer. He also understood that being Caribbean gave him an advantage, because he could read these texts with a richer insight. There are those who can't understand how my ancestors made the cultural fragments that were left for them post-slavery into a fantastic tapestry. They think that this is glorifying slavery. It is not. It is defying it. The irony of C. L. R. James was that he found respite from colonial oppression in the works of so called 'dead white men':

> In Shakespeare I had the clash of passion and lust and love and revenge and friendship and all that, that I could see around me with ordinary people.[2]

He understood that the best people to filter the Caribbean experience were Shakespeare, Sophocles and Shelley. And equally that the best way to unpick these writers is to see them through the post-colonial experience. The idea that a black child could be 'oppressed' by reading Homer or Shakespeare is patronising. And it is the reverse that is true – Homer and Shakespeare can inspire and liberate black children.

So here was C. L. R. James, the writer of *Black Jacobins*, extolling the virtues of an English classical education. Sadly, I didn't get all of that good stuff from my comprehensive experiment. But thanks to Sunday school, and teaching myself at the library, I had all the basics in place by the time I went to university. Having furthered and refined my studies at university, I have found this education in the canon a wonderful and inspiring guide as an adult with a career, and it is this foundation that is key to any successes that I have had.

In 1995 I completed my PhD at the University of Nottingham, looking at the connection of masculinity and school performance. After my studies, I became a teacher and a university lecturer, being awarded a CBE in 2016 for my contributions to education. In 2004, I set up a charity called Generating Genius. Based at Imperial College, London, it was designed to fast-track black boys who loved science and technology into the UK's top universities. We worked with them over five years, starting at the age of 14. Essentially, I wanted to give these students the alternative education I'd received in Penge. One project was to take ten boys from a Caribbean background to Jamaica for a science summer camp at the University of the West Indies, where they would team up with ten local boys. They had the time of their lives doing high-level science on a campus where everyone looked like them. The project was filmed by Channel 4 and later screened as a documentary. Most of the students went on to top universities and are now high-flyers in their careers. Was this programme successful because the boys finally saw great black role models, successful people who looked like them? When we spoke to the students afterwards, they all said not really. For them, the best thing was that they learnt independence, living away from their parents. This was a rites-of-passage project in which – as we say in Jamaica – they learnt 'to walk good'.

On 26 January 2023 I was officially made a life peer in the House of Lords. I only wished my parents were alive to see how a poor boy – born in Brixton, raised in Penge – got to put on that big red robe and call himself Lord Sewell.

Like most people, I love wearing 'crowns' and getting honours – not least because I know that all of them have been given to me on my own merit. My mother used to say to me that I was born to do something special; these were great words of encouragement. I knew that my ancestors had put in all the hard work, and that I was now running around enjoying the freedom they fought for. I am not naive or insensitive to the realities of racism and other oppressions, but nevertheless I have decided to seize the time. After my introduction ceremony, one of the doorkeepers said to me that he was so happy to see someone who looked like him joining this esteemed chamber. I entered the Lords with my head held high.

Here is my maiden speech to the House of Lords:

My Lords, I thank you all for the opportunity to give my maiden speech during this debate on lifelong learning.

Before I start, I must confess that my wife and daughter have warned me severely that I should not tell any jokes, because they claim you will not find me funny – a bit like dad dancing – so I shall try to refrain. I was also told to refrain from any football metaphors. That said, I am sure that many of you have been curious about this new signing: will he freeze in the penalty box or will he be the new Erling Haaland, able to deliver 50 goals a season and help my party to victory? As my mother would say, only time will tell.

I start by thanking noble Lords across the Chamber for taking me in in my first few weeks. I know many of you smiled as I pretended to know where I was going. I give a special call-out to the doorkeepers, who have been particularly friendly to me, with a great sense of humour – especially the ones from south London. I am also grateful to my noble friends Lord Godson and Lord Mendoza for introducing me to the House and for their continual mentorship, which has been really helpful.

My parents came here in the 1950s, as part of a group of Caribbean pioneers hoping to make some money, then go back home. They did not, as a false myth would have you believe, come here to help build back Britain. They were not on some noble mission to save the mother country. However,

34

like many, they stayed on, and soon owned their own home outright while supporting their relatives back in Jamaica and their own children here in the UK. If my parents were alive today, they would be proud of my achievements so far.

The idea of lifelong learning is appropriate, given my long-standing work in education. I am a trained teacher, a teacher trainer, an education researcher and a consultant. In 2002, I was lucky to be part of the board of the Learning Trust in Hackney, the body that took over the miserably failing Hackney education authority; I would like to link these comments with my friends Mike Tomlinson and Alan Wood. At the time, we faced an authority that was deemed not only the worst in Britain but the worst in Europe. Led by those two – as I said, I was grateful to be part of that team – we turned it around within five years. It became, as noble Lords know, one of the best authorities in the country, with the authority's flagship Mossbourne Academy, which led to the academy movement that we know today. I am really proud to have been part of that movement.

STEM – science, technology, engineering and maths – subjects are key to the country's development. Back in 2004, I had the foresight to create a pipeline programme, starting with 12- year-olds and developing them during the school holidays into a new generation of talent. I called that charity Generating Genius. It led to thousands of young people from poor and black backgrounds studying STEM subjects at university. In fact, when I visit Oxford colleges and hear a south London accent and wonder where it is from, it is often a student from our programme. It is encouraging to know that and to see their fruition – and the noble Lord, Lord Blunkett, spoke a minute ago about starting early and building up.

The other key aspect of the programme is that we give young people fantastic career development by exposing them to a range of opportunities that their schools would never have the capacity to do. We have recently made the decision to share the programme across all income groups, across the country, from Hastings to Hartlepool.

In 2021, I chaired the Commission on Race and Ethnic Disparities. Using data from the Office for National Statistics, the commission disrupted the usual narrative and showed that many of the disparities in education, employment, crime, policing and health were founded on multiple and complex factors based on class, geography, family structure, and individual and group agency. I am happy to say that the Government accepted all our recommendations and produced an excellent policy document, *Inclusive Britain*. Racism persists on all levels; I am proud that the recommendations are delivering sensible solutions.

I now see my work as helping to champion a group that has been marginalised, misunderstood and maligned. I am talking about the British small farmer. As a fledgling farmer myself, I must declare my interest. We need to ensure that farming is linked to our developments in science, particularly in hydroponics, and the other green technologies that we in this country are at the forefront of developing. We need to make farming a real skill and aspiration for a new generation.

I am also interested in the need for skills development in young people. In the past, the cry was, 'Education, education, education' – I dare say that it occurred across the House. The cry that we are all embracing now is, 'Skills, skills, skills'. What emerged from my so-called race report was a recommendation for the Office for Students, the university regulator, to stop universities offering poor-quality courses or face tough regulatory action. We need more students doing vocational-related degrees, particularly those from under-represented backgrounds.

As a farmer, an innovator, a developer of STEM skills and a change manager, I hope to make some humble contributions to the work of the House. I look forward to working with all noble Lords in this great Chamber of revision and scrutiny.

MAKING PENGE A POLICY

So, when thinking about educating young black people, what lessons can we take from my life?

Most obviously, I would say that there are three myths around education that swiftly need debunking, before they do us any more harm. They are often bandied about and seem more prevalent now than at any time before.

Myth number 1: It's twice as hard

The idea that black people who were successful in schools like mine had to work twice as hard as their white peers is a myth. None of us worked hard at school, because nobody expected us to. At school we were surrounded by white working-class failure; our peers were hardly the great achievers. The environment was one of demoralisation and failure, in which working hard was looked down on.

This idea of black people having to work twice as hard comes from two places: the old rags-to-riches, pull-yourself-up-by-the-bootstraps narrative, and the notion that black parents would say to their children: 'The world is against you, so you have got to work harder, to beat the white person.' I am not saying black parents never said this – they did, and they do. But I am saying that I never applied this so-called 'wisdom'. I was never convinced by this advice. If I had believed that the world was stacked so much against me, then I would have likely just given up. I wouldn't have been inspired to work harder.

My mother's advice was much more convincing. She simply told me I was a genius. When I worked hard, it was not because I wanted to battle against a white world that I perceived to be against me. I worked hard when I could see a reward.

Myth number 2: The curriculum is too white

One of the myths about school in the 1970s is that our curriculum was white, classical and European, with slavery the only black history taught. The theory here is that if we had learned more black history, we would have been given the confidence to do well.

If only. We didn't roll out of our comprehensives with a full classical education, extolling the virtues of Greece, Rome and the European masters. Our schools were unaccountable babysitting spaces, and many students left without qualifications. The reality is that what many low-income children lacked was a knowledge of anything. Black and white children in failing state schools didn't learn much at all.

On the other hand, I was able to get on in life precisely because, as a younger man, I delved into the classics. The poetry and plays of Shakespeare, the *Iliad* and *Odyssey* – these cornerstones of a traditional education in the humanities leave any young person equipped with skills, values, and insights that they will draw upon for the rest of their life.

Myth number 3: You can't be what you can't see

We are constantly told that ethnic minorities can't be what they can't see. But there were very few black teachers in the UK in the 1970s, and none of them were at Kentwood. There were no black Lords that I knew of. Even today, the likelihood of being from an ethnic minority and having a black or brown teacher is low, even in schools that are majority non-white. So how do any black people achieve anything? According to Berkeley linguistics professor John McWhorter:

> The teacher bias argument ... falls down when we consider that black students generally do not perform appreciably better in schools where they are taught by mostly black teachers. A friend of mine is now teaching in a functioning public school in a big city with a mix of working class and middle-class black children. He found himself facing the same lack of commitment to school that we hear about so often ... and yet all of the teachers are black.[3]

I found this when I went to teach in Jamaica. Outside of a handful of elite prep and high schools, the black majority were failing in core subjects like Maths and English. These children only had black teachers and leaders, yet primary and high school failed to deliver. The race of a teacher is not as important as the quality of the teacher, and the school system that they are in. When it comes to education, identity is not as important as competency.

Moreover, the reality is that most black professionals simply do not choose to be teachers. If we keep telling kids that they have no likelihood of succeeding without black teachers, they are going to feel as though they are sure to fail. This is a terrible message. If your success depends on somebody else's existence, if you are always relying on somebody else to turn up, then failure is likely. We need to tell children that their academic success is not up to somebody else – it is in their hands.

In place of these damaging myths, I am convinced that success revolves around three factors:

1) Flipping a narrative of negativity into one of positivity – for instance, my mother calling me a genius.
2) Welcoming, rather than fearing, excellence – for instance, encouraging young people to read the great literature that is every English speaker's right.
3) Recognising the power of human agency to influence our current conditions – not focussing on external factors that children can't control, such as the race of their teacher, but rather zeroing in on the truism that by applying themselves to their learning, all children can achieve great things.

These three ideas run contrary to the usual narrative on black success. That story too often starts with black people running counter to the so-called 'white mainstream'. There are fantastic stories of people becoming musicians and athletes, having done things 'their way'. But the average person is not going to be a chart-topping singer or an Olympian. We shouldn't infer a trend from what will always be an anomaly.

To continue the sporting metaphors, when a football team starts to lose matches, we don't encourage them to take up cricket. We tell them to improve. Not so, seemingly, when it comes to black children, where we repeatedly hear it said that the reason they are doing poorly is because the education system doesn't cater to them personally enough. The knock-on effect of this has been disturbing. We are dumbing down the standards required, on the grounds that black children are too fragile to clear the bar. This is completely the wrong way around and runs the risk of becoming a self-fulfilling prophecy. If children believe that they need black teachers and a 'black curriculum' to succeed (or indeed white working-class teachers and a white working-class curriculum), they may well end up becoming too fragile to clear the bar when these things aren't present. All the while, elite private institutions will continue encouraging excellence and expecting the highest levels of attainment. Should we be surprised when they get it? Should we be surprised when a gap opens between those who study the classics and those who are told implicitly that it isn't for people like them? Should we be surprised when young black people become demoralised, demotivated, and stop recognising just how much potential they have?

The most remarkable thing happens when we read Tolstoy, or Jane Austen, or Homer. A long-dead author, who lived in a time, place, and culture very different from our own, reaches out of the pages, and through history, and we recognise them. But this requires highly developed critical faculties – the key product of a great education. I want black children to have the opportunity to see themselves in Tolstoy, Jane Austen, and Homer. I want them to see that they are classics for a reason – they have perennial relevance. Unfortunately, by being so literal-minded about everything, we run the risk of making significant only that which is directly familiar. This isn't to say,

'No James Baldwin, only Shakespeare'. We can have both. The reading of one is enriched by the reading of the other.

My formal education didn't necessarily set me up to have the successful career that I have enjoyed. But then, my career, like my education, was also a product of my environment. I became known as a writer and thinker due to my work at *The Voice*. And it's there that we go next, with my time at university finished, in the post-riots London of the 1980s.

2

FINDING MY VOICE
GARGOYLES AND SPIDER GODS

M Y favourite of the Jamaican folklore gods is Anansi, the spider god.[1] He is the hero of numerous folktales, stories taught to children. Anansi is sometimes the victim of the powerful, and at other times he is an antihero who scams the less fortunate. But most of the stories show Anansi in the same way: he is greedy, ambitious, clever, and cunning. He can't bear to see anyone get ahead of him, and since he cannot win by strength, he depends on guile. He is a two-headed (and eight-legged!) beast. His stories are powerful tools to have in your knapsack as you go forward into the world. They were shared in Jamaica, having their roots in Africa, and can be seen as a framework for resilience, resistance and accommodation in the face of a cruel and racist world. We all need, at times, to be a little more like Anansi. But there's a morality tale here, too: Anansi can also be the villain, who learns the hard way.

It was to Anansi that my mind turned when I first encountered the memorable scene in *The Rainbow* by D. H. Lawrence where the heroine, Anna, is taken to Lincoln Cathedral by her

43

husband, Will. He wants to impress her with the grandeur and stone-captured spirituality of the building. Instead, she falls for the gargoyles on the side, the rebels who give reverential religion the finger. Lawrence writes:

> These sly little faces peeped out of the grand tide of the cathedral like something that knew better. They knew quite well, these little imps that retorted on man's own illusion, that the cathedral was not absolute. They winked and leered, giving suggestions of the many things that had been left out of the great concept of the church. 'However much there is inside here, there's a good deal they haven't got in,' the little faces mocked.
>
> Apart from the lift and spring of the great impulse towards the altar, these little faces had separate wills, separate motions, separate knowledge, which rippled back in defiance of the tide, and laughed in triumph of their own very littleness.

The gargoyle is an unexpected, paradoxical figure – traditional, yet subversive at the same time. Gargoyles are part of the establishment, but they (literally) stick out. The building also needs them. They are carved into the architecture of old churches, usually taking the form of a grotesque animal or human. Often they were attached to the gutter system of the roof, with their mouths acting as spouts for rainwater, thereby helping to keep the masonry from being destroyed. In short, that magnificent, soaring cathedral needs that mischievous gargoyle.

Like Anansi, they do something positive and effective, and yet they can be beastly. There's humour here, but it's of a sharp-tongued kind. Humour, irony and cunning are great tools – we associate them with jesters and artists, but they are also the tools of the survivor. The Jamaicans were spot on to make the trickster a comic figure who challenges the given order. The horrors of slavery and colonialism had made them past masters at how to undermine the powerful and circumvent the traps.

Above all, and like Anansi, the gargoyles are both in and outside the system. The gargoyle has been traditionally misunderstood as simply a practical and decorative addition to old churches. In fact, they speak to us about how we engage with the orthodox, the traditional and even the oppressive. They speak to me because they speak to a number of representative features of black success. Black success is part of the orthodoxy, but it is also slightly separate. It is mischievous, practical, satirical and defensive.

In my own life, I have always felt an affinity with these characters. I was both in and out at school, at university, and then, later, when I started my career. My formal education had finished, but my education in life was just beginning. As I explained in the previous chapter, the reasons for success are not always what we think they should be. And a great example of this – one that has had a profound impact on my own life – was the success of *The Voice*, the controversial newspaper that emerged from the rubble of the 1981 riots and became known as the black *Sun*.

FINDING OUR VOICE

Bold and loud, fierce and fearless, *The Voice* opened its mouth in East London just after the Brixton riots of 1981. Prior to this, the only black news-sheet that had any sizeable readership was the British edition of the *Jamaica Gleaner*, Jamaica's bestselling newspaper. The *Gleaner* was geared to my parents' generation and full of news from 'back home'. It barely acknowledged a black British generation and only increased our alienation: we were invisible not just to the British papers, but to the Jamaican ones also. Britain was ready for a new outlet that told the black British story without the racist bias and poor journalism. Many black people read the tabloids, the *Sun*, the *Mirror* and the *News of the World*. We needed a paper that had all their wonderful style and appeal, but without the racism and sexism.

The Voice's founder and owner, Val McCalla, was born in Jamaica and was part of the wave that came over to Britain in the 1960s. His achievement was to identify the emerging culture of the black British identity and to hone it into tabloid form. Helped with start-up money from the Greater London Council – then in its radical, Ken Livingstone era – his paper quickly established itself as an important campaigner against all forms of racism. For local authorities and voluntary organisations concerned about the lack of ethnic minorities in their ranks, it became a valuable recruitment tool. There were pages of job advertisements.

McCalla saw that Britain's national press gave scant coverage to black issues – and that when it did so, the result was usually negative. He saw that the *Jamaica Gleaner*, with its news from 'back home', was boring to the younger generation. There was a new generation that needed a British voice – and the best fit for this would be a popular tabloid newspaper.

The Voice was to make Val a millionaire, and allowed him to indulge in his other grand passion: horse racing. Former *Voice* columnist Dotun Adebayo speaks of his pride at seeing Val roll up to the Brixton office in a massive Mercedes and his door being dutifully opened by his white chauffeur. Anything like this was unheard of in Brixton at the time. The paper would go on to be a massive bestseller and one of the UK's most successful businesses.

While Val's contribution to black British publishing is undeniable, his entrepreneurial nous also struck a chord with others outside the community. Recognising that the use of colour was an integral part of any self-respecting tabloid, he persuaded his Lincolnshire-based printers to invest in state-of-the art colour printing technology. It was a gamble that paid off handsomely for both parties. The striking new-look *Voice* would provide a valuable template that the printers' were able to wheel out to impress existing customers and attract new ones.

I worked at *The Voice* from 1985 to 2000, most of the time as a freelancer. I had a degree in English, and had been a decent teacher of English in schools, so surely it would be an easy switch to journalism – right?

The only positive about naivety is that it contains a kind of confidence. I was about to get a rude awakening.

The Voice were informally recruiting black writers and they set me up for an interview with Val. I knew nothing about how to write news stories or the framework of a newspaper. Channelling my inner gargoyle, I thought I could try and con him by going in as an overconfident black bohemian. I wore a smart trilby hat, long scarf and big overcoat, and I'm sure it made an impression. The office thought I was some kind of black 'exotica' flown in from New York or Paris, rather than simply getting the bus in from Lewisham where I lived.

Val was not interested in my flamboyance. He was, however, interested in my link to Jamaica. The fact that I had taught

47

there, and was clearly a patriot, went down well. McCalla still had a passion for the old country, and wanted to be surrounded by those who flew the flag. I got the job and started the next day.

To some, Val came across as a shy man who never sought self-publicity.[2] But not to me. With me, he was *far* from reserved; in some ways I believe he saw me as the son that he always wanted, and ended up quasi-adopting me. No, that's not quite right – he was more like a Renaissance patron. He asked me to write two books while I was still being paid a salary. He, much like his organisation, was an Anansi-like figure.

The first assignment was a commemorative book to celebrate the 100th anniversary of the death of Jamaican national hero Marcus Garvey. It was 1986, so we had a year to get the book written, published and launched to hit the 1987 deadline. Marcus Garvey was a fascinating figure who managed to create the biggest black nationalist movement in history. This was worldwide, and challenged all the dominant ideas on colonialism and racism. His big idea was that the world had been chunked up into racial/national domains from Asia to Europe, so it was time that black people in the diaspora returned to develop a power bloc in Africa. He started an organisation called the Universal Negro Improvement Association. Its biggest membership was in America, where Garvey based himself after leaving Jamaica.

It was clear that my generation in the UK had only heard of Garvey as a kind of folklore figure. Few really understood his story and significance, and it was similar in the Caribbean and America. He should have been on the curriculum in schools, certainly in Jamaica, and there is an argument that he needs to be studied alongside figures like Martin Luther

King and Winston Churchill. What we realised was that if we were going to make his story popular, we had to use all the methods of tabloid journalism. Too many black history books had been bland tracts that would never reach the mass of the people. We needed great pictures and lots of human interest stories. So I approached the book as if it were a news story. We also saw that if the book was to sell, we needed to make it about Garvey's legacy as much as his biography. This would allow us to make the book global in scope and to roll out all the historic black celebrities who had been influenced by his teachings – people ranging from reggae singers Peter Tosh and Burning Spear to Kwame Nkrumah, the first president and prime minister of Ghana.

The book sold out, and even had an American edition. Val funded several promotional trips to Jamaica and America. I still see the book, *Garvey's Children: The Legacy of Marcus Garvey*, in libraries across the world.

I have been truly surprised by the number of people, from government ministers to community workers, who tell me that the book transformed their lives. And it taught me an important lesson about black success. It was our emphasis on fun, accessibility and making things relatable to the mainstream that gave the book its popularity. So many black history books are so gloomy, or end up in a long, complicated and highly debatable route back to Egypt, where black people were the real heroes, supposedly. We did away with all the nonsense and told Garvey's story in a way that connected with the interests of ordinary people. I got my first real taste of channelling my inner gargoyle. To be both inside and outside the mainstream. To use humour and wit. To be commercially minded.

LIVE AND KICKING

The Voice had – and would always have – a complex identity, incorporating a range of people and voices. Some black people were outraged at *The Voice*'s style of presentation. Others found the paper hilarious. At the same time, because of its campaigning style, it was blasted by white conservative Middle England as a radical threat to order, funded by left-wing zealots. The conversations, quarrels and controversies generated by *The Voice* gave me a wonderful opening. It was clear even during the 1980s that there was no uniform 'black community' with a single view on matters. The paper would have to do many things at the same time: it would have to speak to persistent racial injustices and at the same time satisfy the human desire for gossip, entertainment, scandal, black hypocrisy, and the crude madness of life. Black people were not cardboard cut-outs; they lived lives as complex as the rest of humanity.

I was asked by the new editor, Steve Pope, to write a column called 'Live and Kicking'. It would break the mould of the way black editorial had been handled to date. We would not only uncover racial injustice, but also go after the sacred cows within the black community itself, exposing hypocrisy and some of the bland self-righteousness of so-called community leaders. I was allowed to have a field day, and everyone was fair game. The column dominated the paper for ten years.

Steve was, for me, the best editor at *The Voice* and the most radical.[3] He edited the paper in its glory days during the late 1980s and early 1990s. His mission was clear: *The Voice* was going to be a black tabloid and we would cover everything. We would have stories of black youths dying in Stoke Newington police station alongside a 'baby beautiful' competition. What

The Voice would not be was an outlet for those who wanted us to describe our lives as total misery. Pope brought a wonderful sense of agency to the paper: black people were thieving scumbags, victims of racism and poverty, nasty criminals and generous community heroes. They were businessmen and hairdressers and local councillors. Black people were ... people. Real people.

Pope dared to put all our linen – dirty and prim, raunchy and strait-laced – out in public. This was difficult for some in the black community, who argued that papers like the *Mail* and the *Sun* always put out negative stories about black people and that we should counter this by accentuating the positive. We had all grown up with a tradition of white journalism that threw out headlines like 'Coloured man rapes white woman in Lambeth'. What Steve realised was that *The Voice* didn't need to be the 'positive' response to racist journalism. There were plenty of positives in telling a good story, rather than a story of goodness in which the key actors were black. We wanted to show our complexities, contradictions, beauty, kindness and nastiness.

The idea of a unified 'black community' was useful during the 1960s and 1970s, when Caribbean people felt under siege from everybody – from racist landladies to a hostile police force. But *The Voice* became a force in the 1980s and 1990s, and its shift from the earlier idea of 'one community' to something more diverse, and also more mainstream, was what made it interesting and powerful. We were part of Britain but not of Britain – part of the cathedral, essential to the cathedral, but at the same time separate and different.

According to Steve Pope, the paper's left-wing backers saw *The Voice* as a political tool, a mechanism for highlighting black suffering and promoting anti-racism. Steve preferred the old

News of the World slogan: 'All human life is here'. He humbly says that the publisher Val McCalla needs to take credit for the format, while his job was merely honing the vision.

Under Steve's watch, we gave black people a chance to examine and probe their full humanity. Race and racial politics were not enough to explain the complexities of our lives as we transitioned from Caribbean immigrants to British citizens born and bred. During this intense period of about a decade, we helped make Britain a more open society.

What energised *The Voice* in its early format was that people literally came off the street to give us stories. At times, the paper acted as an unpaid citizen's advice agency, where journalists would fix people's problems, usually around housing or employment discrimination. There was always a range of Anansi-esque characters hanging around in reception, each with a cause or a new product to sell. But there were also plenty of regular people who were angry that the council, or the school, or the police had let them down. The paper really didn't have to go too far to get its exclusives. Black people felt confident enough to share their stories with an outlet they felt would listen to, and perhaps even solve, their problems ... or at least promote their various agendas.

For me, as a journalist, my most bizarre community engagement was with a runaway prisoner. This fellow had escaped from Ford Prison in Sussex and insisted that he wanted to see me. He was a keen reader of my column in the prison library and decided that after his breakout his first destination would be *The Voice*. We persuaded him to return to jail and it was decided that I should drive him back. We took a picture of him walking sadly back to his prison complex, and I got a front-page headline '*Voice* Returns Prisoner'. We were not sure what law, if any, he had broken but we felt it was a public good to not let him be picked up by the cops.

There were other public goods, and many real achievements. Pope didn't shy away from the fact that black tenants seemed to face terrible council-housing conditions. He was clear that this was racism, pointing out that a lot of the people who ran the housing offices were white and their attitudes were discriminatory. He saw *The Voice* as being pivotal in changing the demographics of councils, and in consequence, improving their service to black citizens.

But it wasn't all local politics and escaped prisoners. The paper was packed with profiles of old and new singers and actors, many from America but also local talent. *The Voice* was the first to profile Mel and Kim, a pop duo consisting of sisters Melanie and Kim Appleby. The duo reached number one in the UK with their 1987 single 'Respectable', which also topped the US dance chart. They had three other UK Top 10 hits with 'Showing Out (Get Fresh at the Weekend)', 'FLM' and 'That's the Way It Is'. Tragically, Mel passed away at the age of 23 on 18 January 1990, from pneumonia following treatment for metastatic paraganglioma. When her sister was diagnosed with cancer, Kim took time out of her career to nurse her for two and a half years.

I remember them coming into the *Voice* offices, two cheeky East London girls, full of confidence and energy. *The Voice* was proud to break their story before they became big stars. There was also something vulnerable about them: they were about to hit the big time, and yet they were just normal black working-class girls from London.

In those pages, there was real diversity. Looking at the mon-ocultural landscape of modern black media, one feels nostalgia for the old *Voice*. There was cognitive diversity, a plurality of voices that seems to have vanished from black media. In some (ironic) ways, *The Voice* was the original 'safe space': anyone, and everyone, could belong there.

The Voice succeeded because it was able to channel that gargoyle spirit, that blend of the sacred and the profane, the grand and the irreverent. It was funded through recruitment advertisements and by establishment bodies – councils, charities and public sector organisations. But between the pages of adverts for worthy jobs, there was a huge range of stories: political, African, American, music, sport, gender wars, cute babies and one I have never forgotten – a news story about a house in Jamaica haunted by a duppy (ghost) singing a song about *punani* (a Jamaican word, used mainly by DJs, for a woman's vagina). Now *that's* a scoop!

Nowhere was this diversity more obvious than in two columns: mine and by Marcia Dixon.

STIRRING THE SOUL

I was always a fan of Marcia Dixon. She came from a working-class background like me, and her columns were edgy and fun. Marcia, a committed Christian, became the longest-serving journalist on the paper. Her column was called 'Soul Stirrings', and was a must-read for the black church community. The black church would soon emerge as perhaps the most powerful and lucrative force in black Britain, and Marcia was a strong voice within it. She built her reputation at *The Voice* and then cleverly channelled her expertise into creating a public relations agency for black Christians, using Facebook and other social media.

The great thing about Marcia's journalism was that she represented the core ethos of *The Voice* – edgy, campaigning, controversial, funny and full of humanity – but interpreted it in her own way. Her section was a paper within the paper, a black Christian Voice. It even had its own letters page. On scrutiny, our left-wing council paymasters might have seen her evangelical views as reactionary and (as Marx would say) the opium of the people. But they had the good sense to keep quiet. Marcia's weekly pulpit went in for some serious finger-wagging about sex before marriage and damnation for those who didn't repent of their sins. That said, the page wasn't intended to be offensive to non-Christians, it just was allowed to express and celebrate the views of the black Christian community in all its diversity.

The page operated like a gargoyle (provoking, frank and direct) when it came to the subject of sex. It was a column utterly obsessed with relationships. There are more women than men in the Pentecostal church, and this has had some pretty obvious consequences for male behaviour. In a strongly worded column called 'Lead Us Not into Temptation', Marcia pulled no punches in her treatment of a pastor caught with his pants down. The career of the South African anti-apartheid activist the Reverend Allan Boesak was ruined following revelations of his adulterous affair with a white woman. Marcia *did not* hold back. And the Reverend really only got her started. She quickly went gunning for anyone who may have enjoyed a bit of hanky-panky.[4]

Marcia was brilliant at being both of the cathedral (praying) and apart from it. She believed that if you're going to find a husband when the pickings are so small, you've got to make an effort. And that effort, inevitably, is worldly rather than sacred. She had plenty of advice for women: 'get out and about', 'avoid men with Romeo reputations', 'always look your finest' and 'believe that you deserve the best'.[5] The God stuff is often left at the door, and we are given some pretty standard training in self-actualisation. Pray for miracles ... But also, go out and make them happen.

In 1988 Soul Stirrings featured a story about a dating club for Christians, run by Marcia Brown, a member of the New Testament Church of God in Hitchin. For a small fee, Christians would be placed on a confidential register and introduced to other Christians of their choice. Marcia Dixon (not Brown) commented: 'The setting up of the agency is in response to people's needs to form lasting relationships. It's a fact that some Christians, young ladies in particular, are leaving because they become romantically involved with people outside of the church. Marcia is hoping that this agency is one way of quelling the tide.' Both Marcias were determined to keep things pure, but they knew the pragmatic power of both networking and make-up.

I was always interested that Marcia said so little about racism. It would be wrong to say she ignored it or was indifferent to it. But the page served as an outlet for a range of other issues that affected her readership. The church itself was an enclosed community, giving people a power base that they didn't have in the wider world. A security guard, for example, working in a big City bank where he is ignored by all the young go-getters, may be a big-time deacon in his church. In many ways, the church offered a relief from the madness of white racism and a chance for black people to express their wider humanity. But this was no escape hatch from real life: the problems that appeared in the other pages of *The Voice* crept into Soul Stirrings. At the time, there were serious issues for black women who were moving through the social mobility gears faster than black men. Soul Stirrings was a place in which those issues could be aired, understood and even soothed.

What Marcia pointed out were the upstream reasons why the Caribbean community couldn't build on the success of the early Caribbean pioneers. This had everything to do with the collapse of the family. She was really a prophetess sounding a warning to her community that unless we could build stronger families, we would be at the bottom of all the social indicators. Sadly, she was right.[6] Marcia's honesty, although sometimes hard to stomach, pointed to a framework for success that was built on a moral foundations – rooted in getting a good education, getting a job and getting married.

Marcia was both an advisor and an exemplar. She was herself a success, but she also pointed a pathway to success. Today, it's a pathway that can be overlooked. And yet the family values that Marcia highlighted, while perhaps extreme or difficult to live up to, really do have an impact on people's lives. Once again, it was the gargoyle spirit that made it possible – she was able to best maintain the building by being just a little outside of it.

TAKE THE MONEY AND RUN!

The Voice had a strange relationship with the local councils. In a genuine and well-intentioned way, London councils wanted to boost their recruitment of black staff. The 1980s and early 1990s was a period of left-wing local authorities, with Lambeth, Hackney and Islington leading the vanguard of 'anti-racism'. They couldn't really fly the flag of diversity if their own councils did not reflect it in their workforce. They all undertook a massive recruitment campaign, and the best outlet for this was the country's best (and really only) black newspaper. There were times when the paper was so packed with job adverts that you had to wade through the pages to find a news story. My own column, which was meant to be a page, would sometimes be cut by half so they could squeeze in more advertising.

The councils might have paid for *The Voice*, but they didn't own us. Our opinions were our own, and very often in conflict with the left-wing orthodoxy of the councils. In the edition of 3 May 1995, I wrote a column entitled 'Staging the Equal Opps Act: When "anti-racism" does more harm than good'. I analysed an independent report on Islington Council in North London. The report stated that the council was so anxious about black and gay sensitivities that it failed to investigate the allegation that staff had abused children in its care. The report said: 'We are told that managers believed they would not be supported if they triggered disciplinary investigations involving staff who may be from ethnic minorities or members of the gay community.' I never bought into the extreme rhetoric of 'loony left' councils. Much of that was a caricature. However, their leadership too often allowed anti-racist ideology to conceal problems – and even, in this case, serious crime. While I continued to go after the councils, they still wanted their ads on my page.

In my column, I was always questioning the shaky idea of black unity. I knew that most of it was a fabrication, a lie. Take the issue of role models. The argument went that black children were suffering because they couldn't see people who looked like them doing well. If they were only exposed to the greats, they would stop knife crime and fathers would look after their children. In a column of 26 October 1993 called 'The Year of the Reluctant Role Model', I wrote:

> Fashion designer Bruce Oldfield can't understand why certain people expect him to be a black role model. Talking in last week's *Voice*, he refers to a panel discussion where someone asked him to account for what he has given back to the black community. Oldfield said: 'All of us (on the panel) felt that people just had to get out and do it for themselves.'

I pointed out that if a black person had said this back in the 1970s, they would have been despised as a traitor and someone lacking in community spirit. I wrote that black stars could now be placed in two camps: the first was the 'catch me if you can' type role model, and the second was the 'time to pay back' kind of hero. At the time, I placed supermodel Naomi Campbell in the first camp. She had stormed ahead to be the world's best in a very white industry and never felt obliged to leave any ladders for her so-called 'community'. I loved that. We didn't owe her anything and she felt no debt to us. It's not that she lacked pride in her culture or history, but rather that she saw success as an individual effort.

In Britain, we often point to America as the big beast of black unity. However, many have found this 'fictive culture' an oppressive one. My column referred to an article in the African-American magazine *Essence*, where a black student complained about this pressure. He wrote:

> To them [fellow black students] the community was a rigid religion I had sinned against. To them, I had not taken the sacrament of weekday protests and weekend parties. I had

not worshipped at the altar of the black woman, and worst of all, I had joined another church with a white fraternity. These were serious sins from which there was no salvation. But what all these newly minted aficionados missed with their heads buried deep inside Frantz Fanon and Kwame Nkrumah is that Blackness is neither a religion nor a choice. It is a race, culture and nation we are born into and spend every waking moment constructing. We share a history but react individually. There have been as many black selves as black people, all valid, all black.

The student who wrote this shared my frustration at how being black had become like a religion; he, like me, was a gargoyle. We were disruptive commentators on a black ideological edifice that by the 1990s had grown tired. We were hanging outside of the cathedral with our tongues sticking out, fallen angels with no place in the old order.

Given that 'blackness' was close to a full-blown religion by the 1990s, there were many apocalyptic types calling out the pending doom of black youth. They were mainly on the left, and they blamed our plight on the evil forces of capitalism. In one of my columns called 'Cashing in on Materialism', I challenged the late Tottenham MP Bernie Grant, who had said: 'Our young people have been exposed over the last ten years to a climate in which all that seems important is how much you can accumulate, how you can spend it, and where you can spend it. Every day they are subjected to an unprecedented media onslaught which tells them success equals fast lifestyle, fancy clothes and flashy cars.'

Now, Bernie Grant wouldn't have dreamed of going to the burnt-out ruins of the old communist Moscow to tell them how awful it is to have a spanking new Mercedes Benz. The people there wanted more than Ladas and state-issued tracksuits. They had a desire for the fast, the flash and the fancy. And why do the youths of Georgetown, Guyana – Bernie's birthplace – have a fixation about getting to America? It's the same thing. Try telling them that success isn't about making money and spending it. All this supposed evil 'onslaught' from the media, at a time when Guyana didn't even have its own television station. I knew Mr Grant was in church when he made those silly comments, but he should have known better, I said:

> This hasn't stopped the British left cashing in on the spiritual with missionary zeal – the kind that was sold to our forebears in West Africa. The opium of the masses was simple: think of all things heavenly and we'll look after your gold and diamonds. After all, we don't want you innocent children to be corrupted by materialism.

It was great fun exposing the contradictions that often underlay such well-meaning, but pious, platitudes. My column ends with some key home truths on who really cashes in on 'anti-materialism':

> Perhaps the strangest irony of the Left is its answer to the break-up of the family, inner-city riots, badly educated children, alienated young people – in fact every social problem: the word is SPEND.
>
> Yes, good old Mammon will save the nation that is dying from Mammon. Labour's belief is that cash is the cure for all family ills. And this comes from people who criticise the government for reducing social policy to a series of cash transactions.

If money is the answer to all our social problems, then let's cut the hypocrisy about flash cars and clothes. Thatcherism, which the Left saw as the devil, is therefore directly based on its own attitudes – the concept of the consumer nation and the consumer state ... Success has its trappings and it's only the boring (Prince Charles) and the tight-fisted (the Queen) who don't flash it.

CHANGE THE WORLD

The Voice never had sacred cows: it really was open season on everyone – whether that was the police, racists in government or a black leadership that borrowed from America. It was ironic that a black newspaper found itself on many occasions battling the so-called anti-racist ideologies of left-wing councils. The battle of same-race adoption was a prime example.

New guidance from the government came in the wake of Avon County Council removing a two-year-old mixed-race girl from a white foster couple. The council placed her instead with a black mother who was already taking care of eight children. I wrote a column off the back of this claiming that common sense tells us it shouldn't matter what race a parent is – they simply need to provide a loving and supportive home for the child. This went against the consensus. At the time, people thought that black babies must have black parents – even when there were no black parents willing to adopt them. I supported the government's plan to prevent local authorities from banning white families adopting black babies. I wasn't naive about this. I remembered the bad old days of the 1960s, when black and mixed-heritage children often looked ill at ease with their new white parents, especially when it came to the care of skin and hair. This could be solved, though, through proper training and monitoring of the parents. And besides, parents having to learn some new skills at bath time was a whole lot better than a child being stuck in a care home.

This kicked off a big debate in *The Voice*, with letters arguing for and against same-race adoption. What I found most moving were the letters of those who suffered in care homes. They tore into the local councils for being so fixated on race over the possibility of finding a loving family. Of course, the fact that we had this argument raging could have proved difficult to us – we relied, at least somewhat, on the council's advertising pound. But a columnist's job is to say what they think without fear or favour. And I felt that too many councils and lobby groups were ideologically wedded to the idea that a black child being raised by a white family was a fate worse than death. The ideology was powerful, a doctrine as dominant and unassailable as a cathedral. But it led to black babies, locked up, waiting for black families who may or may not show. It was my job, the gargoyle's job, to call it out and lobby for change.

Between 1987 and 1990 the number of black and mixed-race children advertised in the magazine *Be My Parent* tripled. By January 1990, 130 under-fives had waited six months or more for adoption; not one white child had to wait this long. In one case, a child went into care at the age of two and didn't find a family until they were four.

Some social workers at the time argued against transracial adoption on the grounds that white parents leave black children confused about their racial identity. I quoted Dr Jocelyn Maxime, a black clinical psychologist who ruled out transracial adoption: 'I don't care if there are a thousand white families out there,' she said. 'It is better for a child to wait in a caring residential establishment, that could be at least nurturing that child's needs, than go out there and face a situation of psychological mal-health in the future.'

There is no scientific evidence to prove that transracial adoption harms black children – it's merely an intuition. I quoted a study in America on transracial adoption, the biggest to date. It concluded: 'We have seen black children grow up with a positive sense of their black identity and knowledge of their own history. Indeed, 66% were proud to be black. The research clearly suggests that a significant number of white families have raised black children successfully and given them pride in their racial origin.'

Those who argued that white families gave a negative image to black children missed the point. The real issue was that some black children were left in care without a family, while keen white parents were turned away.

The issue of adoption and race came back in 2022, in the government's response to my Report of the previous year. Although we never looked at the issue of adoption in the Commission Report, the government wanted to make this a vital addition. Current data shows that black children are more likely to be in care (7%) and less likely to be adopted (2%), compared with their share of the under-18-year-old population (5%). That said, Asian children are less likely than black children to be adopted (1%) compared with their share of the under-18-year-old population (10%). White children are less likely to be in care (74%) and more likely to be adopted (83%) compared with their share of the population of under-18-year-olds (79%).

The good news is that, in response to campaigns to find more ethnic minority adoptive parents, we have seen an increase in the number of approved ethnic minority adopters, which went up 32% between March 2020 and September 2021.

However, it says on page 64 of *Inclusive Britain: The government's response to the Commission on Race and Ethnic Disparities* (March 2022):

> Maintaining continuity of the heritage of their birth family is important to most children; it is a means of retaining knowledge of their identity and background. However, social workers should avoid placing the child's ethnicity above other relevant characteristics when looking for an adoptive family for the child.
>
> Agencies must not delay placing a child with the prospective adopter simply because they do not share the child's ethnic or cultural background. Many adopters provide brilliant love and care for children with whom they do not share the same ethnicity.

The government went on to develop its own action on adoption and race disparities. It was keen to increase the number of black children adopted and reduce the time they have to wait to be adopted. This would mean allowing ethnicity not to be a key driver for potential adopters. They heard the cries from the cathedral wall.

THE VOICE GOES QUIET

If *The Voice* provided a bridge between the old folks from Jamaica and the new black Britons, the journalists who worked there lived in that same liminal space. Many made the transition to the mainstream. Some left journalism. Steve Pope could easily have gone on to edit a national newspaper, but he decided to retire. With this exception, everyone I knew who worked on the paper went on to have a successful career in mainstream media. Former editors Onyekachi Wambu, Kolton Lee and Sharon Ali went on to be top television producers. Former sports editor and deputy editor Richard Adeshiyan also enjoyed a successful stint in television, before going on to launch *New Nation* newspaper as its founding editor. He would go on to reinvent himself as an influential PR guru, notching up an impressive list of high-profile clients on both sides of the Atlantic.

Afua Hirsch and Joe Harker were soon mainstream names in television and newspapers. Lesley Thomas is now the weekend and beauty editor at *The Times*. Prior to that, the talented Kathy Watson became editor of *Woman's Realm* and published two great biographies. Then there were the Adebayo brothers, Diran and Dotun. The former is a novelist and a lecturer in creative writing, while Dotun is a BBC radio presenter with his own show. What is interesting is that few wanted to stay writing exclusively about black people's interests: they wanted something broader. One such character was Martin Bashir, who went on to do the infamous interview with Princess Diana. How many people knew he used to work the sports desk for *The Voice*? There's a wider lesson about black success here: black success is success full stop. People who unlock the power of agency use it to spread their wings. They won't forget where they came from, but they also know where they're going.

After Steve left *The Voice* in the early 1990s the paper became isolated from its communities. Sales took a nosedive with the coming of the internet and social media. Suddenly 'citizen journalists' on Facebook and podcasts were competing for the attention of readers. The paper as we knew it was finished. It still exists, but only as a monthly publication and *The Voice Online*. In the era of online citizen journalism, opinion-making has shifted to social media. *The Voice* is now just one of a myriad of black voices.

While this chapter no doubt shows my nostalgia, the demise of *The Voice* is no tragedy. It reflects a changing community living in a more open Britain. On the one hand, a new black generation was emerging, no longer just Caribbean but African. On the other, mainstream newspapers like *The Guardian* began to carry many stories about black people's lives and experiences.

After the death of *The Voice*'s publisher, Val McCalla, in 2002, the *Jamaica Gleaner* took ownership of the paper – a piece of poetic irony if ever there was. They paid too much at a time when newspapers had already been usurped by the internet. Every time I travelled to Jamaica, I would drop in to see the late Oliver Clarke, the white Jamaican who owned the *Gleaner* empire. We became good friends over the years, and he liked my work. Oliver admitted that he had overpaid for *The Voice* and it had become a burden. The paper brought in little advertising and had little credibility in a changing British landscape. However, he felt that he couldn't just let it crash and burn. The paper was now designed in Jamaica, and Oliver would send trusted lieutenants to oversee operations. Talk about a reversal. Here was a black British news outlet being controlled by a white Jamaican who found it difficult to understand the British context.

That said, credit must be given to the *Gleaner* for having the guts to buy the paper. There was a real sense that they had a moral obligation to continue the legacy of a great African-Caribbean product, which was founded by a Jamaican. Those who took it over wanted the paper to be accepted by establishment Britain, and at the same time wanted it to be a voice of resistance. These two conflicting desires came to a head weeks before the death of Queen Elizabeth II. The paper had landed a massive scoop by getting the then Prince Charles (soon to be King) to be their guest editor for a special 40th anniversary edition.

Speaking about the publication, Charles said: 'Over the last four decades, with all the enormous changes that they have witnessed, Britain's only surviving black newspaper has become an institution and a crucial part of the fabric of our society. This is why I was so touched to be invited to edit this special edition.'

When Charles agreed to his guest editorial stint, he was probably unaware of how little influence the paper now had. A new generation of black Britons, mainly from a West African background, had never heard of the paper. That is why the arrangement suited both parties: the monarchy (guilty of its colonial past) needed to reinvent itself, and the phantom *Voice* could do with the boost of royal endorsement. In the event, *The Voice* received many letters from old readers saying that the paper had betrayed its values. Twitter accounts were firing with rage; Facebook groups lamented that *The Voice* had finally lost the faith. One example of this was a letter written to the *Jamaica Gleaner* by Hackney community activist Seymour Mattis:

This is my response regarding Prince Charles editing *The Voice* newspaper. Without fear or prejudice, I am just letting you know that I am a Jamaican and proud of my nation.

I cannot understand why Prince Charles, who has a heritage of a colonial past, would be deemed as appropriate to edit a black newspaper.

Prince Charles's ancestors, King Charles I and King Charles II, were directly responsible for initiating chattel slavery in Jamaica and other parts of the Caribbean, we all know who benefited and the impact it had on black people thereafter ...

Until these wrongs are righted, I do not see how Prince Charles, linked to a colonial past, could be a suitable candidate for editing a 'black newspaper'. Something clearly is not right![7]

The Voice had miscalculated. They saw Charles's involvement as a PR stunt that would make people talk about the paper again – and show that it had great contacts in high places. It backfired. The paper was linking itself to a monarchy that was already having credibility problems about race (Meghan Markle). Looking back, it is clear that by the time the *Jamaica Gleaner* bought *The Voice*, the paper had outlived its usefulness. It had successfully accomplished many of its key goals and it would have to radically reinvent itself or gracefully retire. On the positive side, *The Voice* was a trailblazer. It showed how to be a success. It gave confidence to a new generation of black voices – a true plurality – to promote their identities, politics and perspectives through online content.

Steve Pope is dismissive of the intellectual pontificating of today's black identity politics, which he claims is a middle-class obsession. He insists that the majority of black people show little interest in such pronouncements, and prefer to speak about everyday human matters. *The Voice* in its heyday managed to capture this 'everyday humanity'.

I am not sure what replaces it, but *The Voice*'s lessons of entrepreneurship, agency, and community engagement are a great legacy – as is its sense of fun. In the 1980s it sometimes felt as if we were inside a black church, a cathedral even; we were there for a variety of reasons, ranging from tradition, to racism, to a simple liking for the music – but we seemed to have lost a sense of the wider world. Once the internet and YouTube appeared, the citizen journalists splintered into a variety of interests and causes; we would never be quite the same.

The Voice gave young people of my generation the skills and confidence to get out and succeed in that world. The last word should be given to Marcia Dixon, who, for me, really captured the essence of the *Voice* project. Marcia, in a recent blog, said:

> I took a trip down memory lane when I wrote this blog for *Woman Alive* about receiving an MBE for my work in the faith community.
>
> I had forgotten that I was a student when I started writing *The Voice* newspaper's Soul Stirrings column. I was studying Social Science at South Bank University with a view to becoming a social worker. Writing for *The Voice* put paid to those plans.
>
> I was reminded of how much people valued my Soul Stirrings column – it was the go-to page for anyone who wanted to learn about what was happening in the black church community.
>
> And I recalled some of the great people I interviewed during the course of my working life including the Reverend Jesse Jackson, Baroness Valerie Amos, David and Carrie Grant, James Cone, the father of black theology, Bishop Wilfred Wood, the UK's first black bishop, the Winans (my favourite gospel group), Karen Gibson (long before she sang at the Royal wedding) and many more.
>
> I loved writing the Soul Stirrings column. It was work I loved, and I remain grateful for the opportunity to write about the black community issues of faith and gospel music.[8]

Like Marcia, I loved writing my column. People would tell me that when they opened the paper they would go straight to my piece, even if they disagreed with everything I said. I worked within the spirit of the paper, which was to call out racial injustice, but also reflect the wide range of interests of our readership. Black Britain was evolving rapidly. Generations were coming up that no longer looked to the Caribbean or America for authenticity. On the other hand, we were also kings (in London) of the black diaspora; nowhere was there such a marketplace or intersection of world black cultures in one space. Britain itself had to come to terms with a swiftly changing population, and at times its institutions failed to keep up. *The Voice* provides a vibrant history of that change.

My column adhered to traditional values of decency and fairness. It exposed self-appointed black leaders when they fell short. It was clear to me that emerging alongside a genuine struggle for racial justice were race hustlers. They needed – and still need – a narrative of victimhood in order to keep their jobs, receive grants and stay relevant. Sadly, this hasn't changed – there are new books and films released seemingly weekly that revel in black misery. They have become a new racial establishment, a new cathedral, which means well but keeps us from looking out to a new open Britain. The lesson and legacy of *The Voice* is that we should never be prisoners of an orthodoxy. This means speaking up in ways that may not always be popular.

At the same time, it's not enough to be forever on the out-side looking in. Racism is real, and it affects black people. My argument does not seek to minimise this truth. But having a will to succeed is real, too. Agency is real, and it is something the individual can cultivate, rather than simply hoping for something outside them to change. Legendary figures from my time at *The Voice* epitomised this agentic character: Val McCalla, Steve Pope, Marcia Dixon.

It was precisely this character that I sought to cultivate in the classroom as a teacher. And it was this North Star that I kept in mind when, just a few years after I left *The Voice*, I found myself a member of the Hackney Learning Trust, tasked with turning around some of the worst schools in Britain.

3

CUTTING THE GORDIAN KNOT
THE HACKNEY LEARNING TRUST

Turn him to any cause of policy,
The Gordian knot of it he will unloose,
Familiar as his garter ...

—Shakespeare, *Henry V*, Act 1: Scene 1

I N 2002, as a new member of the Hackney Learning Trust,
I sat in a meeting feeling as though I was back at my old
secondary school in Penge. Although I was from the relatively
soft suburbs of south London, and Hackney was a watchword
in the media at the time for inner-city decline, there were
obvious similarities: lack of discipline, poor exam results, and
black children faring worst of all.

The new board, me included, had been brought in to change
things. There were two very different expectations of how we'd
do. Weary of yet another intervention, those who had been
around Hackney politics for many years thought we would
fail within six months. But inside the Trust itself there were
high expectations of a new dawn. The board members were

73

volunteers from education, business and civil society. I was chosen because of my work on black boys, *Black Masculinities and Schooling: How Black Boys Survive Modern Schooling*, published five years earlier. When I saw the data and the massive hill we had to climb, I wanted to scratch into my brand-new desk, like many a schoolboy before me: 'Get me out of here … this is f—ing madness'.

My position on these matters went against all the consensus on race and education. I was bold enough to say that black boys were trapped by family collapse, youth culture and poor school leadership. There was resistance to my view from an education establishment that refused to tackle these realities. I feared that the Hackney Learning Trust would face the same kind of pushback. And even if we were going to tackle these issues head-on, surely they would take decades to fix?

I was wrong. Within a couple of years, we had transformed our schools. Hackney had risen from the worst education district in the country to being among the best.

This chapter is the story of how we achieved this transformation, and what lessons it teaches us about black success.

When the Learning Trust first started, I was acutely aware that the majority of students were leaving primary school barely able to read and write. And when it came to secondary schools, the majority left at 16 with few or no qualifications. The schools in Hackney reminded me of my own comprehensive school, Kentwood Boys. There, outside of a small, selective group, most students only worked until Wednesday. On Thursday and Friday, they hung out listening to music in the music room. This was not an attempt to expose students to Bach and Beethoven. It was simply that the teachers had given up. The big question people were struggling with was:

how do you educate working-class boys? Writing in *The Voice* in March 1996, its editor said:

> The problem facing white working-class boys is now becoming as glaringly obvious and acute as those affecting black pupils. And in the main since we share the same schools and neighbourhoods. Perhaps it is also to forge alliances with them ... How we make this into a board-based educational campaign against low expectations and low achievement is the big question.[1]

In many ways, the failure of black students shone a light onto a comprehensive system that was failing all low-income students. Above all else, I thought, the schools in Hackney were wasting talent. The poor results in Hackney, especially for black children, came from a context of low expectations and schools that were a law unto themselves. The result was that, in the 1990s, the London Borough of Hackney had some of the worst educational outcomes in Europe. We will concentrate on just one school: Hackney Downs.

The story of Hackney Downs started well; it was one of East London's best grammar schools in the 1960s. The school had illustrious alumni, such as Nobel prize-winning playwright Harold Pinter, actor Steven Berkoff and athlete Dalton Grant.

In 1969 it voted to become a comprehensive, and in September it opened its doors to a non-selective cohort, in the process admitting some of the problems of this deprived inner-city borough. By the time it was closed by the government in 1995, Hackney Downs boys' school had a reputation for fighting and exclusions. Setting off the fire alarm was a regular game; sometimes it happened several times a day. This not only disrupted lessons, but allowed students to clash in the corridors as they rushed into the playground. It was a place where well-meaning teachers struggled to get the boys to listen and learn, fights occurred in the classrooms, and teachers were regularly absent with stress disorders. Most of those involved in the breakdown of order were African-Caribbean boys. Some had been excluded from other schools. Many were angry. Many had special needs. The minority who wanted to work found the behaviour issues of their fellows so nightmarish and distracting that they were unable to do so.

In 1993 the school expelled 25 students over ten days for violence. The day that headteacher Ken Russell wrote to parents to say that he would now be excluding fire-alarm offenders, the school hit the press because of a fight with a neighbouring school. Just before its closure, over 70% of the boys spoke English as a second language, half came from households with no one in employment, and half the intake had reading ages three years below average. African-Caribbean boys were the lowest achievers and had the highest rates of school exclusion.

The council that ran Hackney schools was shambolic. Flicking through the headlines of the 1990s, you get a picture of an utterly dysfunctional Labour council, locked in a series of internal wars. There were claims that party chiefs were racist and demanded sexual favours of office staff, while also being involved in financial corruption. Meanwhile, all the chief actors were preoccupied with internal backbiting and squabbling. What was missing was a focus on the dire exam results of black children in the borough. Who said what to whom at a council meeting four years earlier made no difference to a mother whose child would leave a Hackney primary school barely literate. In 1995, the then Conservative government described Hackney Downs as 'the worst school in Britain'. They closed it.

The decision to close the school was key for the Learning Trust. It freed up space for a new school, but it also represented everything that had gone wrong for black pupils in Britain's education landscape. While I have sympathy with the view espoused by some at the time that there were worse schools than Hackney Downs – which eventually became a dumping ground for pupils expelled from other schools – the fact remains: it was an abject failure.

Despite the controversy, the decision to close Hackney Downs and open Mossbourne Academy on its site nine years later has proved to be the right one – for students and for the borough. Mossbourne's combination of tight discipline, silent corridors and loads of homework has made it an academic success. The first of the academies, it provided a template for a new type of comprehensive school and gave new opportunities to children from disadvantaged backgrounds. The academy model led to significant improvement in black academic achievement.

LESSONS FOR HACKNEY

In the days leading up to the closure, I sat in the Hackney Learning Trust offices, reflecting on everything I knew about education. My own schooldays, my research into black boys and education, my horror at what the data in Hackney was telling me, the tumultuous, headline-making closure of the school – all these passed through my mind. I was about to help shut down one of Britain's worst schools and kickstart a brand-new education policy. The academy system was to begin with its flagship school, Mossbourne.

To appraise the Trust's work, let's look at the data for Hackney as a whole. One of the key numbers for me was the performance of African-Caribbean students during this transformation period, as collected by the Learning Trust:

- In 2006, 50% of Caribbean-heritage pupils achieved Level 4+ in Key Stage 2 English and Maths; by 2011, 72% were achieving Level 4+ in both KS2 English and Maths, an improvement of 22 percentage points.
- Over the years 2006-11, Caribbean-heritage boys' attainment has increased by 24 percentage points (43% in 2006; 67% in 2011).
- Between 2006 and 2011, the percentage of Caribbean-heritage pupils achieving 5+ A*–C grades, including English and Maths, has increased from 28% in 2006 to 45% in 2011 – an improvement of 17 percentage points over six years.[2]

I feel so honoured to have been part of this success. But how did we pull it off? More specifically, how did we raise the education outcomes of African-Caribbean children and other ethnic minorities, when no one else could? How did we stop making 'diversity' and 'deprivation' a millstone or an excuse in the journey towards academic excellence? How did we turn Hackney into a place of pride for all children – and more specially one that could deliver great results for African-Caribbean children?

The Learning Trust focussed remorselessly on school leadership. It created a school improvement team led by outstanding former headteachers. An exemplar was the late Tricia Okoruwa.

She arrived in Hackney as a teacher at the struggling De Beauvoir Primary School in 1992 – a time when Hackney schools were at the bottom of national league tables. Tricia became the headteacher at De Beauvoir Primary in 1999, and joined us at the Learning Trust in 2004. Our strategy was to find headteachers who had turned failing schools around. We then placed them on our wider school improvement team. This team set challenging standards and targets for each school in Hackney, ensuring they became good or outstanding in a decade.

Tricia progressed from leading the primary strategy to becoming director of education when schools were returned to Hackney Council at the end of the Learning Trust's contract. Long before educators decided to pursue phonics as a key national strategy to improve literacy, she led the way with her campaign 'Get Hackney Reading'. The strategy was not based on assumptions about cultural deficits or 'decolonisation of the curriculum'. Hackney school libraries had a diversity of texts, yet its seven-year-olds were still bottom of the class when it came to reading. Children didn't read because they *couldn't* read. Tricia developed a no-nonsense, no-fuss, no-excuses strategy to get them learning. She had high expectations of the teachers and provided the support for them to deliver. If they didn't deliver, they had to go.

The other key executive leader we recruited during my tenure was Steve Belk. He joined the Trust in 2003, with a record of delivering results as headteacher of the local Stoke Newington School. We nabbed him from Lewisham, where he was their head of school improvement, and appointed him executive director for learning and standards. Steve ran a clinical regime. As the board, we were given a traffic-light coding system that signalled the condition of every school in Hackney. Headteachers were brought in to explain why their school was on amber or red. In many cases it was a signal that they needed to fall on their own swords: the quality of school leadership has a direct relationship to the quality of learning outcomes. Getting highly competent headteachers into failing schools worked. We soon reached a point where most schools in Hackney were good or outstanding, according to OFSTED. Poor leaders think that the outcome you're seeing is inevitable. When you replace them with leaders who expect high standards from everyone – white, black, rich or poor – outcomes improve.

When I share this success story with those out of the borough, they ask me what interventions we used specifically with black children. The Learning Trust sponsored a number of schemes of this kind. However, most were a waste of time and cash. The key intervention in the late 1990s was the Ethnic Minority Achievement Grant (EMAG). The Grant was given to councils that had significant numbers of ethnic minorities. It was the Labour government's big idea for reducing under-achievement in black children. It had two aims: to support students for whom English was a second language, and to aid in 'black achievement'. But the grant was often poorly used. The government gave most of the money directly to schools, leaving the Education Authorities with only 15% of the allocation.

When it came to telling schools how to use the money for students with English as a second language, the guidance was clear: schools were given great examples of how best to use the support teachers. Simply put, these students had to learn English. After they did, we could see that they *flew*.

But when it came to the guidance for African-Caribbean students who didn't have a language issue, the picture was confusing and patronising. There was a bit about monitoring racial harassment and making the curriculum more inclusive, but these things did nothing to close the achievement gap.

The guidance also gave some good-practice examples from schools that allegedly were doing wonders with African-Caribbean children:

Once the Head felt that a degree of consistency had been achieved, he introduced a weekly behaviour focus for pupils. This included things like:
- Line up quietly outside the classroom before lessons.
- Think twice before you speak once.
- Be kind to each other.
- Bring all your equipment to school.
- Walk quietly in the corridors.
- Be polite to non-teaching staff.[3]

It went on to give an example of a school where senior managers would stop children in the corridors and ask pupils what the behaviour focus was for the week. Pupils who knew the answer were rewarded with a chocolate bar. It was claimed that African-Caribbean achievement soared because of this intervention (or as I like to call it, bribe). One must also assume that the rates of obesity rose, too, as students stuffed themselves with chocolate. Yet there is no evidence that children behave better because of such 'incentives'. The irony of this advice from the Department of Education is that quiet corridors and strong discipline would be the hallmark of the academies and Free Schools that would come in soon – yet there they would be achieved by quite other means. The idea that you bribe children with chocolate goes back to discredited child-centred theories, where adults were seen as getting in the way of the free-flowing learning of children. There are no punishments, only rewards for saying and doing the right thing.

On the other hand, as a teacher, I remember African-Caribbean boys telling me that they preferred the strictest teachers in the school. At first this seems counter-intuitive. Surely young inner-city children would love to be in a classroom where they faced less surveillance and fewer demands from teachers? The opposite is true. Students hate the anarchy of a teacher 'who can't control us'. They make the key point that strict teachers obviously cared, whereas those who let behaviour slide did not. They also recognise that strict teachers create an environment in which work can be produced. This speaks to a truth well known in education circles: children need strong boundaries, and they need those boundaries to be consistently enforced.

It wasn't surprising when researchers Audrey Osler and John Hill[4] concluded that although there had been some success in closing the gaps between ethnic minority achievement and national averages since the introduction of the Grant, these had been largely limited to groups receiving English as an Additional Language (EAL) support. They went on to say that the relative achievement of some groups, notably black Caribbean pupils, had not improved at all. Thousands of pounds were being pumped into raising the levels of black Caribbean achievement in schools, but there was no evidence of improvement.

What they wouldn't admit was that the money was being wasted on pet projects like Black History Month and vague race-relations training for teachers. Quite simply, too much money was being spent on identity issues or self-esteem programmes, rather than the nuts and bolts of academic achievement. If you think about it logically, why would this work? If you wanted someone to become an elite runner, you would find them a coach and a training plan and get them out running. You wouldn't take them away from the track to talk about their feelings. When you focus on what matters, you get results. The reason that the English language part of EMAG worked was that it focussed on the meaningful and the tangible; it gave children the language skills that made it easier for them to access the curriculum.

When it came to English-speaking African-Caribbean children, there was no evidence that getting teachers to do anti-racist training would reduce exclusions from school. Once again, this is not to diminish the reality of racism, or to say that every teacher was a virtuous paradigm of the multicultural ideal. Many had written off their black students before they set foot in the classroom. However, too many stakeholders didn't want to confront the real cause of underachievement. This is splendidly articulated by Farrukh Dhondy, a former multicultural commissioning editor for Channel 4 television, who in 1999 wrote in the *Times Educational Supplement* about the need to look wider than institutionalised racism in schools to find the cause of black underachievement:

> The other possibilities need a hard and scientifically passionate examination. It has never been done. Instead we have notions about 'culture', 'role models', 'stereotyping', 'positive images', 'low expectations' and 'unwitting racism' floating about which are grasped from the latest fashionable ethos and put into play in every circular discussion of the wretched subject.

He goes on to ask:

> Doesn't any institution want to draw up some correlative
> tables about class conditions, family conditions, details of
> parenting, cultural pursuits at home, amount of homework
> done, behaviour in class, voluntary attention span, respectful
> and polite behaviour, however animated and lively, and the
> great goal of achievement? [5]

If black history and anti-racism training doesn't explain the
success in Hackney, then what about black teachers? There had
been much talk linking black underachievement to a lack of
black staff and headteachers. During my time in Hackney, there
was no significant increase in numbers of black teachers, though
I did see a good number of black primary school heads who
were fantastic. The actual evidence shows a predictable pattern.
African-Caribbean children excelled where teachers had high
expectations, maintained good discipline, and treated children
with fairness, regardless of what colour skin they themselves
had. The Learning Trust saw significant improvement for black
children without any major increase in black staff. It's clear to
me that definitionally a good teacher is 'anti-racist' because
a teacher committed to the success of their students cannot
discriminate. We put the cart before the horse when we focus
on buzzy anti-racism initiatives and don't plough money into
improving teacher competency.

In fact, during my time, an all-black Seventh Day Adventist
school in nearby Tottenham had to close because of poor
standards. John Loughborough School was a voluntary-aided
black school. In 2013 it closed because its results were so
poor. Headteacher Dr Edwina McFarquhar was professional

and well-meaning, but the school was not viable academically or financially. She pleaded with Haringey council to give the school another chance to show improvements in exam results. At the closure meeting, Haringey councillor Ann Waters, the cabinet member for children, said: 'I think we all feel we have children at the school who are going to be let down if we do not close John Loughborough and move them to another school … We care deeply about the children at the school and in Haringey we want to make sure they get the best start in life. You have asked us to give you another year but I'm afraid we are out of time.'

Although there was a clamour for all-black schools, changes in the curriculum and more black staff were not factors in the great achievements of black students in Hackney. How then do we disentangle the question and find an answer?

THE GORDIAN KNOT

According to legend, Alexander the Great's army entered the Persian city of Gordium and found an ancient oxcart tied to a post with an elaborate knot. Its yoke was secured by what a later Roman writer described as 'several knots all so tightly entangled that it was impossible to see how they were fastened'. According to Phrygian legend, whoever could unravel the knot would become the ruler of Asia. After contemplating the Gordian knot for some time, Alexander decided to cut through it with his sword. And that was that. He eventually conquered Asia as far as the Indus and the Oxus rivers, fulfilling the prophecy.

In Hackney, we likewise faced a Gordian knot: no one could figure out how to teach poor inner-city children. Teachers either loved such children to stupidity or, back in my day, brutalised us with the cane. The oxcart was and is the great barrier of low expectations: in Penge, no one really believed that we could do as well as our middle-class, privately educated counterparts. Ironically this belief was baked most deeply into some of our most liberal teachers. The oxcart soon became 'white racism', which was said to occupy the heads of white teachers and prejudice them against black pupils. We forgot about fundamentals like good behaviour and doing homework. Instead, thousands of pounds were spent on anti-racist training for teachers. Black children were told they lacked self-esteem, and only once they gained it would they be able to buckle down and study.

This is something we see in many other areas of life. Leaders come into an organisation and try to untie the knot but end up inadvertently making it more secure. Yet there is a simple, elegant solution staring them in the face that they somehow don't see – cut the knot! In Hackney, no one wanted to admit failure. Nobody seemed able to do the basic things or see the obvious weakness. No one wanted to seriously challenge the schools and their poor leadership. Instead, we had lots of distractions, usually focussed on race or masculinity. The argument from many of those wanting more men in the classroom is that boys lack appropriate role models, which female-dominated primary schools cannot give. This argument is very popular in relation to the achievement of black boys.

In 1995 the black US academic Spencer Holland was invited by Hackney MP Diane Abbott to share the findings of his intervention 'Project 2000', a Black male teacher mentor scheme that was having a dramatic effect on the academic performance of Black primary school children in the poor areas of Washington DC. Holland was asked to share his scheme with parents, teachers and the local education authority officials in Hackney, which had similar problems to those of Washington – namely high black male exclusions from schools. According to Holland, most six-year-old black boys in Hackney came from households with single mothers. The boys were rejecting school because they linked learning with being 'anti-masculine' – a link that was reinforced because all their teachers were women. He said: 'The boys do not find it appropriate to be copying a woman. In 1988 we conducted an experiment in a local elementary school. We wanted to find what would happen if we put all the six-year-old black boys alongside a black mentor. These men were all volunteers and from a variety of backgrounds. Soon teachers were saying that their classes had improved – the boys were following the male lead and began doing well.'

My sense is that Holland is right to look to male models to respond to cultural and family breakdown. This was definitely an issue for black boys in Hackney. However, to suggest that these mentors be a constant in the classroom to support female teachers missed the problem. The boys had issues outside the classroom, and what we really needed was mediation mentors who could help families going through particular kinds of stress. Moreover, Spenser's programme would never get past a predominantly white female liberal teaching force, who saw his message as sexist. Some might argue that these teachers, like the boy's mothers, were blocking the avenue to an ideal masculinity. But I am against this black Superman mentor model. Replacing female with male mentors in the classroom sidesteps the real issue of family breakdown. This was the view taken by the ex-leader of Hackney Education Authority, Gus John:

I have no problem with the idea that mentoring could enhance pupils' learning. I have a problem with the thesis which says that it is impossible for a woman to teach boys values and attitudes that get them focused upon learning. I find this part of the thesis difficult to accept ... You are training men to stand next to female teachers and present an alternative authority figure to these kids.[6]

In Hackney we were fighting on many fronts, including poor leadership in schools and family breakdown. My sense is that African-Caribbean boys did suffer a particular trauma because the male authority figures in their lives were problematic. But this is where our understanding of authority figures and masculinity gets badly tangled; we think, like Spencer, that to compensate for 'female classroom authority' we need black male mentors. This, of course, misses the upstream problem of family structure. Some black women were able to compensate for this better than others. However, many of these families needed professional and psychological interventions. No one was practising family therapy with this group; when I suggested this, I was told that I was blaming the victim.

What is interesting is that it would be another black group in Hackney, the Nigerians with their strong family structure, who finally made it to the promised land. The African-Caribbean group were led back from the abyss, and through a laser focus on school improvement we saw them going beyond the national average. However, in the Learning Trust we laid a path for the West African groups to turbocharge into the top universities. This success was powered by their strong hierarchical family structures, where adults are godlike – an attitude that their boys transferred into the classroom. In the post-2000 years I saw how Nigerian children thrived in the traditionally structured Academies, where schooling returned to rituals, rules and rites of passage. For many African children, this was home from home – whereas too many African-Caribbean children were still in the space of 'race and relationships', unable to dutifully accept the authority of school. No wonder that in Hackney (and indeed across London) we saw West African children with better GCSE results and lower exclusion rates compared to their African-Caribbean or mixed-heritage classmates.

So, is having a male authority figure in the lives of black boys a key to success? Yes, it is. What we did in Hackney, by raising the bar for all children, was to boost African-Caribbean results to a record high. I think we would have gone further had there been political leaders willing to admit that we had a family crisis that needed professional support.

In the event, Holland's programme was kicked out by teachers in Hackney. It was yet another kind of intervention that missed the key problem: far too many six-year-olds in the borough simply couldn't read.

The oxcart blocking our way was built by leaders with low expectations. On the one hand there was a snobby elite in its ivory towers who thought we could never get our tongues around long Latin words. But perhaps more sinister were those on the left, who thought that working-class children would be harmed by all this elitism. A third group on the oxcart were the Afro-eccentrics, telling us that we couldn't move on until Britain had paid up for slavery. This meant that the curriculum and teachers needed to be 'decolonised' in a deprogramming exercise that would exorcise all the white vestiges of Empire.

None of it is true. What we needed were well-run schools filled to the rafters with good teachers, whether male or female.

The students needed to learn the basics: reading, writing, mathematics. They needed teachers who cared about them, who were willing to enforce good behaviour, and who were themselves accountable when they weren't up to scratch. The answer was obvious. We needed to cut the rope – do the obvious things – rather than trying to come up with new techniques to untie it.

STRUCTURE LIBERATES

The motto for Mossbourne Academy, the new school built on the ashes of Hackney Downs, was a Latin phrase meaning 'Structure Liberates'. We believed that the laissez-faire, child-centred approach to schooling would not work for our students. The 'structure liberates' ethos aims to free children from a culture of poverty through discipline and routine. According to Mossbourne's first headteacher, Michael Wiltshire:

> Children who come from unstructured backgrounds, as many of our children do, and often very unhappy ones, should be given more structure in their lives. So it means that the school in many ways becomes a sort of surrogate parent to the child, and the child will only succeed if the philosophy of the school is that we will in many ways substitute and take over where necessary. Therefore we want staff who commit themselves to that ethos. It's not a nine-to-five ethos, it's an ethos which says the only way that these children will achieve is if we go the extra mile for them. We have extension classes, we have enrichment classes, and we have Saturday mornings, etcetera … Because that's the only way it's going to work. The

other thing about structure which, again, underpins this philosophy, is that if they come from unstructured backgrounds where anything goes and rules and boundaries are not clear in their home, we need to ensure that they're clear here. So we run very tight systems here, you could call it a traditional approach or a formal approach.

Alan Wood, the CEO of the Learning Trust, would probably laugh if he were compared to Alexander the Great, but he and his chair Mike Tomlinson accomplished what many others failed to do before them: they cut through the crap. Ours will go down as one of the most significant turnarounds in modern education history. Here was an education authority labelled as one of the worst in Europe – and in less than ten years it became one of the best in the UK.

There was so much that I had in common with Alan Wood. He had come from a working-class background and ended up in a school not too dissimilar to Kentwood Boys. His mentors were men who had fought in the war and retrained as teachers. For Alan, they provided the high expectations and discipline he needed as a lively teenager in one of the toughest parts of London. He did well, got his O-levels and went into the sixth form. For him, Hackney was personal because he had grown up in the East End of London and went to school in Stepney Green. He appreciated those teachers who had seen his intellectual capacities and pushed him. Alan's politics are interesting, because he would be no poodle for Labour or Conservative. He has a healthy contempt for the madness of the extreme left and little time for the pompous out-of-touch fools on the right.

The chair of our board, Mike Tomlinson, was a down-to-earth, plain-speaking Yorkshireman; as a former chief education inspector for schools, he understood the workings of central government and commanded respect from the sceptics in Hackney. Mike had little time for bureaucratic niceties. His mission was 'the good of Hackney children'. Headteachers who didn't get this were ruthlessly culled. He was a towering figure, with the directness of a Geoffrey Boycott. Many of Hackney's incompetent headteachers decided to throw in the towel.

Alan Wood tells the story of a visit he and Mike Tomlinson made to two Hackney primary schools. The first of these was a 'rundown 1960s prefab school'. They arrived and were greeted by the headteacher, who immediately said that she wanted them to meet the staff and the students. 'We ask her about issues, she says she needs more staff development courses for her teachers ... We then go down the road to another primary in a better building and nicer learning environment. We had to find our way to the reception, which was difficult, and then we were taken to the headteacher's office, which was tucked away. She complained about everything. No resources, no staff and then says she has only two years left before retirement ... can't we just leave her alone for two years?' Alan Wood said no, and they arranged for her to leave earlier. She was replaced with a better head with higher expectations and more professionalism.

Alan's journey out of East End poverty via education meant that he cared. He simply would not tolerate low expectations, particularly for black children. However, I never heard him or Mike come up with anything that was specifically about race. The only time I heard Alan ever mention the subject was when he said to me: 'Tony, I really hate when white people try and tell black people how to be black.' I hope he remembers those profound words. This attitude meant that he was ready to cut that knot with a mighty sword. He was going to transform the lives of black students in Hackney by changing *everything*. He didn't need to promote special interest groups. He would raise expectations for *all* children in the borough. Alan wasn't downplaying the reality of racism – but he knew black success would come when you raised the tide for all boats.

Alan and Mike understood that the real problem in Hackney had little to do with race relations, but lots to do with the incompetence of the council. It was here I realised that for years black communities had been sold a dummy. The drive for excellence was not going to be achieved by putting our energy into the headline-grabbing politics of identity. We needed to focus on the boring bread-and-butter matters: efficiency, high expectations and accountability.

The Trust operated efficiently because, once a policy or resources decision had been made, we got on with the work of implementing it. There were no second thoughts or last-minute lurches motivated by short-term political expediency – unlike on the Labour-led council.

Alan Wood recalls:

Between 2002 and 2007, I met with over 20 school leaders specifically to discuss their performance and, as a consequence – through one mechanism or another – they left the school where they were headteacher.

The leader of the local Headteacher's Association, Sean Flood, observed at a meeting of heads in 2014:

Alan was never willing to keep quiet about underperforming leaders. There was one period when I spent more time with him defending heads than I did with my staff.

It was a scorched earth policy, taking out the old and introducing the new. One new school was, appropriately, built on land that had been used in a film set for the TV series *London's Burning* – a drama about a team of firefighters.

Talking of firefighters, there's a metaphor here for black success. Firefighting is dependent on there being a fire. It's better to create an environment where a fire is unlikely to break out. That's precisely what happened in Hackney. Asked to explain our success in the borough, Alan Wood wrote:

1. We had a clear vision of what we wanted to achieve;
2. We were given the time necessary to achieve our vision;
3. We were able to appoint first class leaders, not only in schools, but at the Trust;
4. We were willing and able to make tough decisions;
5. We were innovative, and remained relevant; and
6. We were not prepared to let economic deprivation become an excuse for underachievement.

By 2012, 83% of parents were putting a Hackney secondary school as the first choice for their child after primary school.

It was great to see black students succeed in Hackney after decades of poor performance. Once we embraced the goals of high achievement and excellence, there was no holding them back. Today, I can see elements of the Hackney Approach in Katharine Birbalsingh's school, Michaela, and in Brampton Manor School (which we will visit in another chapter). 'Inner-city school' is no longer a euphemism for educationally failing black schools.

Richard Hardie, who was chair of the Learning Trust from 2007 to 2012, summed up our approach:

94

The Learning Trust Board has seen its role as removing obstacles from the path of Trust staff, headteachers and governors, trusting in their expertise and allowing them to focus on improving standards. It is this approach which has allowed education in Hackney to flourish.[7]

Many of the obstacles we removed had been placed there with good intentions. But they had become a distraction, like the Ethnic Minority Achievement Grant, which only worked when it helped young people acquire enough English to access the curriculum.

We had a blueprint in place for how to improve a school, but for me this wasn't enough. I wanted to shoot for the stars. I wanted to find out if we couldn't simply turn failing schools into good ones. I wanted to see how far we could push our best students. Black students were succeeding in Hackney, but I knew there was so much more potential out there. There were students whose talents could take them to the very top of their fields. There were, I was convinced, scientific and mathematical geniuses flying under the educational radar. It was my mission to spot them and bring out their latent talents.

To do so, we needed to follow the instructive lead of a Jamaican sports coach – and his most successful charge.

4

GENERATING GENIUS
SIX STEPS TO SUCCESS

THERE are areas in which black success has never been a surprise and is rarely contested. The fields that immediately spring to mind are popular music and sport. These successes often come attached to a simplistic explanation that locates black people's success in some kind of natural physical gift or prowess. This can be something as ridiculous sounding as 'natural rhythm' or as seductively scientific as 'fast-twitch muscle fibre'. However, as with many of the stories of black success, the truth is elsewhere.

Let's start with Jamaica. On any statistical reckoning, it is amazing how a country of just under three million people should have both the fastest man and the fastest woman in the world over 100 metres. The achievement is not the domain of a handful of great stars, a few one-offs. The Jamaican dominance in sprint was born over a century ago, came of age at the 2008 Beijing Olympics, and has held ever since.

Beijing saw Jamaica win ten gold medals overall. In the women's 100 metres sprint, gold, silver and bronze went to

Jamaica. Top of the 2008 pile was Usain Bolt, who won three medals. A true phenomenon, he went on to win Olympic gold three times and has earned his status as the greatest sprinter in history. In subsequent Olympics, Jamaica continued to haul in the medals.

An argument used to explain Jamaica's success is the widely quoted fast-twitch muscles theory, which scientists claim enables black athletes to run faster. Athletics consultant Jon Entine wrote: 'Bolt and his Jamaican teammates are members of a tiny slice of the world population – elite athletes who trace their ancestry to western and central Africa – whose body types and physiology have been uniquely shaped by thousands of years of evolution to run fast.'[1] There is a gene, ACTN3, associated with these fast-twitch muscles and it is dubbed, fittingly enough, 'the sprint gene'.

It was American 200- and 400-metre legend Michael Jordan who also popularised this dubious genetic fairytale. Just before the 2012 London Olympics he presented a persuasive documentary entitled *Survival of the Fittest*, which linked modern sporting prowess to the slave trade. It argued that the greatest Caribbean athletes had this fast super-gene, which they inherited because the slave owners chose only the healthiest to be shipped to America and the Caribbean. Given that Jamaicans were shipped from Nigeria and Ghana, and given that genetic testing shows that ACTN3 turns up abundantly in the population there, it does raise the obvious question: why, then, are West Africans such slowcoaches? To date, no Nigerian male has ever won a sprint medal.

The reason for Jamaica's success in sprint events is in fact an upstream institution: the annual Inter-Scholastic Athletic Championship, known locally as 'Champs'. This is a national high-school sporting event held every March and one of the most important events on the island. Champs is more than 100 years old – it was first held in 1910 – but became popular after 1999, when the boys' and girls' competitions were combined. It is broadcast on national television, supported with massive sponsorship, and has become a hothouse for young athletic talent. Scouts from many of America's universities descend on the national stadium seeking to woo the local talent with lucrative scholarships.

At its heart, Champs is an inter-school competition with sky-high standards and fierce loyalties. Olympic champion sprinter Shelly-Ann Fraser-Pryce, dubbed the 'Pocket Rocket', ran at Champs representing her school, Wolmer. She still goes to watch the event, gets her nails done in maroon and gold (the school's colours), and stands on a chair, screaming support for the young athletes.

Former Champs competitors often stay loyal to the event. Warren Wells ran in the competition, and was once captain of the Calabar High School team. Now a 200-metre medallist, he shows up every year to deliver an inspirational speech to the boys. The 100-metre champion of 2011, Yohan Blake, is also a former Champs record-breaker, and was once a pupil at St Jago High School. He credits the championship with starting his Olympic career, saying: 'If you look at the world and Olympic champions, you will see a lot of St Jago athletes there, because we know how to preserve our athletes for a career after high school.'

Champs creates an opportunity for young athletes to appreciate the challenges and atmosphere of high-level competition. Fraser-Pryce talks about one of her Champs races: 'When I came out of the tunnel on the track, I was like, "Oh my God!" I remember being so little, and I made the final of the 100 metres.

I came in seventh, but I was proud, because so many people come there and they don't make the final.' She goes on: 'Being at the Olympics later on, I knew that I'd already seen that kind of a crowd before and experienced that adrenaline. As professional athletes, we need adrenaline, but not too much of it.'[2]

There are two factors behind Champs that make it so decisive for future development. The first is that the top schools employ top coaches, which means that young children are exposed to the best training and practice in athletics. The other is an almost religious attachment to your school.

The only reason that Jamaica is able to use its existing high schools as the nursery for top athletes is the obsessive loyalty that Jamaicans have to their alma mater. I have heard 50-year-old women say they would draw blood (their own) for St Andrew's or Immaculate High. Even those who go to schools that are failing academically will madly wave flags of support when it comes to Champs. One memorable moment of school loyalty occurred when top DJ Vybz Kartel was being sentenced for murder. He stood in the dock adorned with the tie of Calabar High School, Kingston, the school from which he was expelled at the age of 16. Above a great story in the local newspaper, the *Jamaican Observer*, the headline read 'Kartel Shows His Colours':

Clad in a white suit, with his alma mater Calabar High School jersey and tie, Vybz Kartel was sentenced to life imprisonment for his role in the August 2011 murder of Clive 'Lizard' Williams in the Supreme Court in downtown Kingston on Thursday.

Despite the possibility of being locked away for the rest of his life, Kartel apparently paid homage to his school's victory in last weekend's Grace Kennedy Boys' and Girls' Athletic Championships at the National Stadium.[3]

I struggle to imagine a British criminal dressed in their old school tie while being sentenced for murder. School tends to be a hated place, with no fond memories. For Jamaicans, your school is an essential part of who you are, and you are hungry to compete with rivals. Fierce loyalty and frenzied competitiveness? That's the ground for developing sporting talent.

The Jamaican model is now being studied by other countries fascinated with this great template for talent development. Assistant track and field coach at the University of Tennessee Ken Harnden says that Jamaica is ahead of most of the developed world with regard to its high-school coaches.[4]

One coach who came through the high-school process was Glen Mills. The *Gleaner* reports of Mills that 'under his watch, Camperdown high school in Kingston became a mighty force in sprinting, and was later dubbed the "Sprint Factory" by track and field fans, as they dominated the sprint events at Champs, Penn Relays and other meets.'[5]

'While at Camperdown, I single-handedly built the track and field programme,' Mills has said. 'I also helped with the development of the football programme. When the school won the triple crown in 1982, I was a major part of the organisation.' After becoming a prominent coach nationally, Mills promised to continue to support his alma mater in whatever way he could.

Mills dismisses any idea that his approach to coaching is 'instinctive'. He reads everything on the science of the body and the latest techniques, to better understand the biomechanics of sprinting. He is a perpetual student, a constant improver. Although on one occasion, on a course run by the IAAF, he found that the lecturer was using him as a case study, and ended up having to study himself!

Despite not being a 'natural', Mills likes to think out of the box. When scouting, he might look at the athlete at the back of the field: he is looking for athletes who are ready to go on a journey of improvement. Almost 20 years ago, he quietly pointed out an individual finishing outside of the medals in a high-school race, seeing something special in a seemingly average performance. The teenager's name? Asafa Powell, who went on to set the world record in the 100 metres twice over.

Mills is also the mind behind the success of world sprint champion Usain Bolt. Bolt approached Mills after he failed to qualify for the 200 metres at the Athens Olympics. Mills isn't really interested in so-called natural ability. He saw technical imperfections in Bolt and knew he had the tools to fix them. It would be a painstaking process of ironing out Bolt's bad habits – a repetitive process that demanded patience and resilience. They would spend hours watching and rewatching video footage, until, finally, Bolt got it right. The medals followed.

Mills is keen to stress the importance of the well-being of his athletes. He recognises that being hot-housed – living the life of intense training – means you sometimes need to let off steam. For this reason, Bolt was never discouraged from going out partying. There were myths that he could eat the worst kind of junk food and still perform. Once again, the real story is elsewhere: he had his own personal chef, but insisted on viewing food as a source of pleasure as well as stamina. The point stands, though: Mills understood that Bolt had to be happy to perform on the track. Having said that, Mills doesn't go easy on his athletes. He's a realist. He knows that one day Bolt's records will be broken. In fact, one of the mantras he repeats to athletes is that they 'must lose in order to learn to win'. It's this grounded, wise and paternal nature that inspires such faith from his athletes.

Just as Jamaican running success is often attributed to the wrong thing – genetics – so too is black success more generally. Black success is not a quirk of blackness, something integral to being black – that's a constrained way of thinking. Black success, like success more generally, is a series of actions and behaviours repeated endlessly. When answering a maths question, there are many ways to be wrong, but only one way to be right. Similarly, the recipe for success is almost always the same, though the ways in which we go wrong vary. The traits, then, of Jamaican sprinters provide a road map for success everywhere, for everyone.

They are precisely the same actions and behaviours that I needed to identify, harness and nurture in my education charity, Generating Genius. In the rest of this chapter, we'll look at the recipe learned from Jamaican sprinters, and see how it can be applied to black success in any field. It is, of course, both very simple and very difficult. There are just six key behaviours that we need to instil:

1. Teach the technique.
2. Set standards high and focus on core knowledge.
3. Be prepared to lose in order to win.
4. Repeat until it's effortless.
5. Give support and investment over the long term.
6. Be a father figure.

Let's take these in order.

1. Teach the technique

On 27 June 2005, *The Voice* newspaper splashed a headline: 'Our Future'. The story beneath was inspirational. A photo showed ten black 13-year-olds in a park, posed in different positions on a huge climbing frame. They looked so innocent; a couple had worn their best ties for the shot. These boys had won a competition, partly sponsored by *The Voice,* to find ten black or mixed-heritage boys who would be the scientists and engineers of the future. This was my idea. The aim was to send a positive signal about a group that, to date, was considered bad, sad and underachieving. The big incentive in the competition was that the winners would be going on an all-expenses-paid trip to Jamaica. Not as a holiday, but as junior students at the University of the West Indies, to undertake inspirational and high-level science. The hope was that this would sow the seed, and that these students would return to Britain focussed on university and careers in STEM (Science, Technology, Engineering and Maths). *The Voice* wrote: 'It is hoped that the programme will help to create a culture of achievement among young black boys.'

That year, 2005, the number of exclusions and poor exam results among African-Caribbean boys remained a huge cause for concern. We needed to change the narrative. The black community needed to see their children's high ability. We needed to challenge the loser mentality that was becoming prevalent. And we really needed to move away from a focus on football, dancing and rapping, in order to see the whole spectrum of talent among young black people. For me, that meant the sciences. Could black boys excel at science and technology? What evidence was there, for or against? At the time, none.

But, like a good scientist myself, I wanted to test the hypothesis that black boys could become scientists and engineers, so I put the thought through the rigours of a real-life experiment.

My hunch was that the British education system was killing off most of our science talent by the age of 12. We gave 13-year-olds the option to choose 'easy subjects' for their GCSEs, and so poor black students couldn't wait to jump away from the hard sciences. It's logical. If getting good grades is seen as the key determinator of success, why take Physics (lots of revision) when you can take Drama (potentially a bit more of a 'wing it' sort of subject)? Girls were also being managed out and discouraged from taking these tough subjects, and the result was that A-level sciences were taken predominantly by middle-class boys.

Currently, even those who choose science are allocated by schools (there is little choice for the student) to either the 'triple award' GCSE science pathway (three separate sciences) or to the lower-status 'double award' pathway (combined sciences). This happens at age 14. For practical reasons, the majority of students in England and Wales are allocated to the lower-status double-award pathway. As a consequence, many are denied the chance of going on to a STEM-based apprenticeship at age 16, as they are deemed insufficiently qualified by employers. Likewise, many students who have the talent to go onto A-levels or T-levels in STEM subjects are rejected by sixth-form providers simply because they were restricted to the lower-status pathway at age 14. These students only have access to non-STEM courses post-16. This has the knock-on effect of exacerbating the UK's STEM skills shortage.

What are the reasons for this bizarre situation? One is that Triple Science causes timetabling complexities that place a disproportionate strain on the whole-school timetable. To offer Triple Science, schools very often turn to maverick solutions (such as extra lessons outside of normal school times), which have a disproportionately negative impact on those who are already at a disadvantage. Because Triple Science needs 50% more curriculum time than Double Science, schools must either magic up the extra time from nowhere, or cram Triple Science learning into the same number of hours allocated for Double Science. Another reason is that many schools have too few specialist teachers (particularly Physics teachers). Removing the triple-award science pathway significantly reduces the Physics-teacher shortage at no cost.

It's worth noting that in England and Wales, Science is the only subject at GCSE with two different pathways leading to two different qualifications of different status; the result is a system that provides *fewer* opportunities for one cohort of students than for another, regardless of the ability of the students involved. No other subject requires teachers to allocate students to different-status pathways to GCSE at age 14, before they even start their studies. This is a bizarre anomaly of the current system.

And that is the position today. Twenty years ago, the situation was even more severe, especially for black children. I looked at the problem in a fresh way. What if there was a huge cohort of black boys aged 12 that had the potential to be great in STEM? What if the weak link was not the boys themselves, but the fact that we don't 'teach the technique'? We put the cart before the horse when we think that black boys 'don't like' STEM. The onus is on teaching professionals to make them like it! So, what would happen if we started working with them as early as age 12 and stayed with them as a protective barrier against negative influences? This would be done by surrounding them with a positive learning environment and introducing them to more Science, Technology, Engineering and Maths. We would create a safe passage for them to realise their talent, a community of like minds, a club for students from similar backgrounds where we would test and nurture their intellectual prowess.

This was the genesis of Generating Genius. It was simply an attempt to teach the technique. Just as Glen Mills taught the strength, conditioning and technical training crucial to sprinting success, Generating Genius was going to ensure that its cohort were actually being taught STEM, rather than an ersatz version. Definitionally, we were aiming high, which, of course, leads us to ...

2. Set standards high and focus on core knowledge

I realised, at the time, that many of the targeted programmes for black boys were making little difference to their educational achievement. They had one thing in common: they were predicated on failure. They were based either on fixing racist teachers or on raising the self-esteem of black boys. But what if neither racist teachers nor low self-esteem was the driving factor?

I was convinced that we had a group of latent geniuses on our hands. Black boys were a sleeping giant who needed to be awakened. This meant that we – black people, and civic society at large – had to have higher expectations of them. They were failing because they had weak family support and, at the time, poor schools. I was appalled that the existing community support was based on the old youth-club model: it was all table tennis and rapping. I noticed that no Chinese or Indian students attended these alternatives. What was far better was the supplementary school model, in which volunteers would work with students, giving them extra lessons in Maths and English.

I wanted to go one step further than the supplementary schools. I wanted to hang on to the students for six years. I wanted to create a pipeline of success that would guide them through their adolescent experience and launch them into adulthood. If they didn't have the luck to come from a stable family background, we had to be an alternative family for them. That did *not* mean a family wholly predicated on race, and it did *not* mean a family offering some psychobabble about self-esteem. We were a family committed to science, to strengthening intellects – and also to moral purpose. Supplementary school had to have some content and some depth: it wasn't just about crowd control. On our programmes, you learned stuff you didn't learn in school. Science for me was the great leveller. Yes, the students knew in the early days that we were targeting mainly black students – but we never did anything 'black'. We simply did Science and Technology. We built robots. We learned about medical research. We got to grips with data. We learned debating skills and how to present scientific ideas. And in doing so we worked with many of the top universities in the UK. We set the bar incredibly high, we focussed on core knowledge in the subjects, and we expected our boys to do well.

This was not the orthodox view. Surely if I was going to support black students, I should have been telling them about the history of Africa and great black inventors? The fact is, many of them *did* know about black history. They needed something else. We encouraged them to look at the successful black present with a view to building successful black futures.

Our decision to kick the programme off with a trip to the University of the West Indies in Jamaica was designed to send a message to students that here was a great university where everyone looked like you. I felt that what they needed was to see their peers from similar school backgrounds hungry to learn about science and technology.

Over the years, my thoughts about the need to see yourself in people being successful have shifted. In America, black students from as far back as the 1940s have not been short of role models or the sight of black people achieving. Yet this didn't automatically translate into a high-achieving demographic. I realised that the Chinese, Indian and West African communities had solved this problem by having the best of both worlds. They immersed themselves in the standard curriculum, no matter how Eurocentric, and this was reinforced by their own culture at home. There has been some awful stereotyping of these cultures. The surprising, but obvious and intuitive, truth is that conservative practices at home reinforce mainstream British school cultures. Students from Chinese, Indian and West African communities are taught to respect authority and hierarchies and to see knowledge as sacred. An *Economist* editorial on China and Confucian education observes that:

> The ancient system of thought emphasises respect for authority, reverence for ancestors and deference to elders. Confucius taught that such values were essential to achieve moral excellence as an individual. Such upstanding citizens would form the basis for wider social harmony and political stability. Emperors used the philosophy to instil obedience.[6]

It's hardly surprising that this small-c conservative view of the world leads to positive educational outcomes. Now, I was not trying to develop a bunch of conformist robots who would accept everything without question, including racism. In fact, our students were the opposite: they questioned everything. That was precisely the point. By giving them the core skills in science and mathematics, we gave them the tools to question the world around them. You can't think from first principles without having learned first principles. That meant there was no way we were going to have 12-year-olds telling us about 'their truth'. We would love and respect them, but we also took seriously our responsibility to teach and guide them. This was clearly lacking in many homes and, ironically, in many schools. Once again, when it came to Generating Genius, we had high expectations, and we focussed on core knowledge.

I realised my young students needed to have a more Confucian outlook. Relationships mattered, just as they did with Glen Mills and Usain Bolt. Looking back, the fact that the programme was led by a black man with mainly black staff *was* significant. In many ways, I became if not a role model, then a reluctant father figure. Not all our boys were from fatherless homes, but a large percentage were. I think it was my absolute belief in their abilities that made the relationship work. Many had not seen an older black man undertaking this kind of nurturing role. It only worked because I genuinely believed they were the best. They never let me down. That's a thing with high expectations – if you expect the best from people, they'll give you the best. University professors would ring me after working with our boys and ask me where I had found such talent – they had never seen anything like it.

Glen Mills's approach to fixing Usain Bolt was never to assume that he was driven by natural ability. What he had to address were technical difficulties – because he had learnt bad habits in his very early days of running. We had to do the same. We had to assume that the boys had poor nurturing at school and in their homes. Our approach was to train all those unused muscles. Usain Bolt spent hours doing squats with heavy weights because this aided the centrifugal force that powered him out of the blocks. He got his body as strong as possible by focussing on the absolute fundamentals. We thought about our students' education in the same way. We built our programme around understanding core scientific principles and knowledge.

3. Be prepared to lose in order to win

Glen Mills's saying that you need to lose to be able to win looks counter-intuitive on first contact. But this resonated for me when I devised a programme for our 14-year-old students at Imperial College, London in the summer of 2010. We were busy doing a coding and robotics project, but I wanted to add an extra degree of difficulty – as well as some social experimentation.

I was friendly with the headteacher of Eton College, Tony Little, and he linked me to his head of Science. As part of the summer robotics programme, I invited 12 of his best 14-year-olds to join us for a day at Imperial. Why would I give an already privileged group of students access to our resources? The students would be asked to work in groups, but the groups had to be mixed. There were six groups with two Generating Genius boys and two Etonians in each. The task was set at the usual high level we expected from our 14-year-olds: build a robot and write coding to make it active. This is the sort of work you do in the first year of a degree.

I inspected the work of the groups and found that the students interacted as if they were old friends. Still, one thing I noticed was the work rate of the Generating Genius students: they seemed to be doing most of the building and coding. The culmination of the programme was a PowerPoint presentation by each group in front of leading Imperial College professors. This was a competition. There would only be one winning group.

What transpired surprised me. All the presentations were led by an Eton boy. As I sat among the judges, I was silently urging our boys to step up and take the microphone. I was frustrated that they had decided to play backing singers after they had done most of the hard work. After the Eton boys left in their coach, I had a debrief with our students. I asked them why they allowed the toffs to take charge of the presentations. They replied, 'Sir, we wanted to step up, but they were so confident'.

At that moment I realised that Glen Mills was right about losing in order to win. We had lost, badly, but I made sure none of the students would forget that session. We ensured that the programme focussed more on debating and presentation skills. From that point on, those boys were never shy in coming forward to lead or present.

The following summer we were invited to an event by one of our sponsors, the French bank Société Générale. We were told that their CEO would be in attendance, because he had heard great things about us. The students decided not only to do a presentation on green technology and finance, but to do it in French. The sponsors were blown away, and we won charity of the year that winter.

4. Repeat until it's effortless

As mentioned above, we took our boys to Jamaica to have them learn among other black children who were succeeding at a high level. What was fascinating about seeing students from the UK and Jamaica working together was the insight into the educational backgrounds of the two groups. It was clear that the Jamaican students were much better at memory-based learning. They knew their times tables inside out and were excellent in short quizzes and memory tests. The Jamaican education system, with its traditional methods of rote learning and teacher authority, gave many of the Jamaican boys an advantage. Their memories were better nurtured.

Katharine Birbalsingh is the headmistress of Michaela Community School, a free school in London that mostly serves lower-income students in Wembley Park. A committed educator of inner-city students and an avowed 'no nonsense' leader, Birbalsingh favours 'traditional' teaching approaches, including rote learning, regular testing, lots of homework and a strict behaviour policy. This approach has garnered a lot of suspicion from left-leaning critics and proponents of 'progressive' pedagogy. Nevertheless, Michaela gets some of the best exam results in the UK, and its traditional teaching approaches have become more mainstream in the education system. I was involved in the early establishment of the school: a group of us would meet in Katherine's front room in Brixton to tease out this wonderful vision.

Glen Mills applied a similar approach of discipline and mastery in his coaching of Usain Bolt. Practice. Practice. Practice. Repetition. Repetition. Repetition. The key to success in figures as diverse as the jazz genius Miles Davis, the superstar sprinter

Usain Bolt, and our boys in Generating Genius: hours of dedicated practice.

At Generating Genius we began to utilise repetition and rote learning as we ourselves were schooled by our Jamaican colleagues. At the age of 12, not only had all our boys learned their Periodic Table by heart, but they understood the concepts too. But we made repetition fun: we used mnemonics and slam poems to keep the boys engaged through the endless hours of practice. With time, they built up a solid foundation, and were able not only to assimilate large amounts of knowledge but to summon it effortlessly, at will.

5. Long term support and investment

For many years now I have been living between the UK and Jamaica. My seafront apartment in Jamaica is just outside the resort of Ocho Rios. One afternoon I set out in shorts and flip-flops in pursuit of some ice cream, when a police car suddenly blocked my path. My heart started beating: there's much talk about bad cops in the UK and America, and Jamaica's reputation is no better. Out jumped an armed policeman with a beaming smile on his face. He came up and gave me a hug.

'Dr Sewell! It's Sheldon from the Generating Genius programme.'

The last time I saw Sheldon he was 12 years old, and now he was nearly 30. I was so pleased to see him. He went on to say: 'Dr Sewell, that programme was the best thing in my life. It gave me direction, purpose and inspiration, it really saved my life.'

Sheldon was now a technical and scientific advisor for the Jamaican police. Right away he demanded that the programme should start again.

'Believe me, sir, Jamaica needs Generating Genius.'

I managed to dig up some old newspaper cuttings, and found a short article on the 12-year-old Sheldon as he was about to embark on the programme back in 2005. It read:

> The death of his father four years ago pushed Sheldon Reid of Knox College to strive for the best in life. Having been chosen for the Generating Genius programme, it seems Sheldon is well on his way to greatness. 'I was overwhelmed as I always encouraged him that education is the way to go, and not with brand names,' said his mother, Karen Doman. 'Sheldon has always been fascinated by the forensic sciences, and watches mostly criminal investigation movies and reads as many science texts as he can get his hands on.' 'Because I like science very much and I want to have a good career, I chose to apply for the programme,' said the teen. This, after his mother saw the advertisement for the Generating Genius programme in *The Jamaica Gleaner* newspaper. The determined teen further added that the death of his father sparked in him a determination to do well at his studies and to achieve greatness. Simply put, he wants to know that his father would have been proud of him.[7]

Glen Mills started working with Usain Bolt when the great athlete was 14, and didn't stop until he retired. The nature of his support changed over time, as Bolt's physical and emotional needs developed, but it was consistent and always had an eye on the future.

Similarly, at Generating Genius we developed a pipeline approach. Students begin aged 14, in a programme called Junior Genius; later they move into our sixth-form programme, and then we have career development programmes and internships while they are at university. Once they have completed these stages, they join our professional network, where they become mentors and role models for the younger students undertaking the same journey.

From an initial intake of 20 boys, Generating Genius developed rapidly into a charity that accepted both boys and girls in ever-growing numbers. We now have several thousand students. We quickly realised that once our students were at university, they had to deal with financial demands often beyond their household incomes. We lobbied for scholarships that would help towards their living expenses, seeing it as a continuation of our work. Just as Mills worked with Bolt throughout his career, we aim to do so with our scholars.

Wasseem Ali is studying medicine at the University of Nottingham, and he also supports our programmes as a mentor and programme administrator. He received a scholarship from one of our partners. He says:

I want to give a prodigious thank you to the Black Heart Foundation and Generating Genius for this extraordinary, life-impacting scholarship! I am beyond grateful for this blessing. Since the age of 16, I have had to work in retail to support my educational needs, which included everything from funding essential educational trips to purchasing textbooks and train tickets for my medical school interviews. Working part-time alongside my A level studies was difficult, and studying Medicine at Nottingham University is proving to be the most significant academic and social challenge yet, especially during a pandemic. I understand what a privilege it is to be able to study this profession, and how hard I have worked to be in my position. Therefore, with the financial stability that this scholarship provides, I can dedicate 100% of my time towards my degree, and so giving me the time to focus on becoming the best doctor I can be. Being able to effectively balance my studies alongside my university's social, volunteering and mentoring opportunities allows me to make the most of my time here, as well as engage in roles that help to support prospective STEM students to achieve their goals. Once again, thank you so much for this support. I strive to repay your generosity and thus contribute to helping future generations of underprivileged students.

Throughout Generating Genius, we run competitions and we give prizes to the winners. However, we realised that because we were targeting low-income students, we should provide free laptops and pay for all their travel expenses to our activities. The great art of motivation is again a kind of muscle memory, because our aim was self-motivation, where students enjoyed our programme not only because it was a ladder to career success, but because it was satisfying. We were teaching skills that matter not just in the classroom, but through the course of life. And we aimed to remain with our students every step of the way.

6. Be a father figure

Glen Mills was clearly a father figure to Usain Bolt, who also had his own father and mother. This relationship was key to their success. As some black communities in the UK struggle to replace the father figure, who is so often missing, the idea of the 'role model' is often heralded as the solution. In 2007, the government announced that 'successful role models for young black men' were to be recruited to counteract educational underachievement and the influence of gang culture. The motivation and intention came from a good place – but it was often hard to sustain such programmes.

The problem is that children, black or white, need exposure to experience and authenticity. The role model who comes to the assembly and waxes lyrical about his own experience is usually forgotten by playtime.

I believe that a contributory factor in the success of Generating Genius was my own father-figure role. I had deliberately constructed a role that would allow the boys, in both the UK and Jamaica, to respect but also fear me. At first, I was uncomfortable in this role, but I sustained it because the boys seemed to like it. I was Mr High Expectations, who would boot them off the project if they dared mess up. My rationale for this came from my days as an inner-city schoolteacher, where boys seemed to have the greatest love and respect for the strictest teacher. These men and women are never abusive; they care for the children. They are the ones who would challenge a student, rather than ignore him, if they saw him doing wrong. They would find the energy and time to stay behind and keep children in detention rather than go home and relax. The boys on the Generating Genius project were all contemptuous of the teachers who allowed them to get away with bad behaviour, but they spoke highly of those who gave them boundaries. These were not the members of staff who acted like bullies or 'shouted' at them.

I therefore constructed a father-figure persona and allowed the boys to have certain expectations of me. The greatest challenge to my fatherly role came from boys who had no father at home. That said, many boys who were brought up by their mums did not find my role problematic. The boys wanted me to play the role of a caring but stern father, and I obliged. They knew that if I corrected them, I was playing a role and doing my job. It was great because they knew I really cared about them as individuals. For some, I became the only significant adult male in their lives.

It might appear that in this book I have used 'father' and 'authority figure' interchangeably. This might worry some feminists, who think I am arguing for a return to a patriarchy. However, I take my cue from the serious devastation that I see in the so-called black family, particularly in Jamaica, the UK and the USA. This really is a crisis of fatherhood and authority. I am not convinced that this is some kind of hangover from slavery. If that were the case, how would you explain the thousands of black men who do take care of their families and do use a condom when having casual sex? The state has not helped with its social interventionist attempts at elevating single motherhood. Nor have we been best served by deliberately ignoring the data on black family weakness, to focus instead on the race activists' obsession with 'white privilege'. Yet every interview with a black boy in crisis in Chicago, Kingston or Brixton will tell you how haunted he has become by the ghost of his father. For him, in a world of chaos, it is this male figure that stands for order and authority within a family context. Everything else seems to be a distraction. By 'authority' I don't mean that the man is some kind of 1950s head of the house. I am talking about moral authority, where the male figure embraces faithfulness, love, kindness and responsibility as key attributes. And as any woman will tell you, he still needs to bring home a serious pay cheque.

Recent studies seem to support the traditional sequence in which the father becomes more important after the age of ten or 11, but this turns out to be dependent on early intimate contact between father and child.[8] Moreover, studies find that fathers who have not understood their own life stories and have not mourned their losses are less engaged as parents. These men are more passive in their thinking and their children less confident and sociable. This can be seen in many black communities, where the cycle of father-need seems to pass from generation to generation.

The difference between flaky role model schemes and the presence of a genuine, engaged significant adult is the way the latter will provide students with boundaries and a framework. These have sacred power. A father figure doesn't merely provide an example, he also picks you up on your mistakes. Children both understand and need this. I had rules that I strictly enforced. I call them 'law lines'.

I am confident that Glen Mills understood the importance of law lines. With Usain Bolt, he managed to perfect a nurturing role in which he offered caring authority. The authority aspect derived from a hierarchical relationship with his athlete – it was Mills setting the training agenda, not Bolt. This resembles something we observe in Nigerian Yoruba culture, where young people on certain occasions are meant to prostrate themselves in the presence of elders. Nigerian children grow up with a sense that elders have an innate authority, which should not be questioned. Contrast this with an African-Caribbean culture, where the fatherless household rate is the highest of all communities in Britain. Many children from such a background question adults' authority and entitlement to their respect. This is not an asset in a schooling context, which is structured around hierarchy. We tell students to do certain things because we are experts in our subjects, and we know how things should be done. This is the way of the world. Those with a sense of hierarchy will be better equipped to deal with the complex hurdles within any school or course of study. By instilling a due sense of respect for authority, Generating Genius has helped to develop the attitudes that help young people navigate their way to academic success.

GENERATING GENIUS TO THE WORLD

My hopes and ambitions for Generating Genius have been realised. This was brought home to me most sharply by a letter received from one of our alumni. She joined Generating Genius at the age of 13.

> The experiences that I encountered through Dr Sewell's Charity were focused on STEM workshops at leading universities and organisations. As one of five siblings, raised in a single parent home within a deprived area which was laden with crime, I was never exposed to opportunities within the corporate world. I had no such connections and no insight into what it was like to even work within the STEM field. As a result, I had never envisioned myself having the ability to work within prestigious and global organisations as I did not realise that I was capable of this.
>
> The workshops that Dr Sewell introduced me to were engaging, empowering, thoughtfully planned and tailored to my learning style. These experiences opened my eyes to what it meant to go to a leading university and organisation, showing

me that with application and hard work it was indeed within reach. The relationships that I fostered with other ambitious students, from a similar background, that Dr Sewell has created as part of the Generating Genius community, were priceless.

With Dr Sewell being hands-on with workshops and engaging in conversation with us, he became a coach. Someone that I could look up to. Dr Sewell and his work helped to foster a self-belief and confidence within me from a young age which was life-altering. He believed in me when no one else did and this helped to drive and navigate me through a challenging educational system.

Despite the barriers and adverse circumstances that were present, his support helped me to make a positive out of negative situations. Today, I have been able to transform my life and I am on the journey of my dreams, now studying to become a doctor at a prestigious university. The positive impact that Dr Sewell has had on my life and what I have been able to achieve because of his influence is invaluable and is priceless. Dr Sewell continues to check in with me now and then and is always happy to offer help in difficult circumstances within my studies.

I would not be where I am today without the crucial support that I received in the early years of my life from Dr Sewell and therefore I am incredibly grateful for his contributions and hope that these can be recognised.

Just before we flew off to Jamaica for the first Generating Genius visit to the West Indies, Kate Taylor, an insightful BBC radio producer, asked if she could do a programme featuring the boys and their parents before they flew out. She would come to Jamaica to catch up on our progress.

She asked me about the rationale of my plan. I said, maybe too boldly:

> We are going to turn the cycle of underachievement; we are going to stay with them for five years. The key point for me is when they are in the labs wearing their white coats and discovering the wonders of science. One thing I'm sure is that once they step on that Air Jamaica flight, they will never be the same again.

The boys seemed to have the same sense that their life was going to change.

What was fascinating was that Kate then caught up with us seven years later and recorded a programme called *Bright, Black and Looking for Work*. Our boys were then 20-plus and just finishing university.

The programme opened with an extract from the 2006 recording. We hear a group of boys answering their names from a roll call, squeaky unbroken voices, like choir boys reaching for the high notes. Embarrassed, the same young men, seven years later, respond to the clip in their matured baritone voices, no longer the cherubs of the past. The contrast is remarkable.

Jamal was 21 at the time of the reunion interview, studying Economics at the University of Kent. The grown-up Jamal laughs at the 12-year-old talking about 'pressure' as he's about to go on an all-expenses-paid one-month trip to Jamaica. The older Jamal says: 'It's funny listening to that clip. There was a lot of excitement on take-off day. Being selected for the programme meant that my talent has been recognised.'

Jamal became a leading City finance expert, working with some of the top firms in the country. All credit must go to his mother, who was not only supportive of our programme but the best role model that Jamal could have.

Boys like Jamal make me feel so proud of the programme. My prediction has been proved correct: all the boys say that this was one of the pivotal events in their lives. Jamal's point about recognition is key. The untold story is how we revealed the boys' talent – firstly to themselves, and then to the world. This was most of the job. When the boys arrived at night in Kingston, Jamaica, they came off the plane wearing yellow tops supplied by our sponsors. The tarmac was full of photographers and reporters, all wanting to see the black boys from England coming to Jamaica to study Science and Technology. We were on the front cover of the national newspaper.[9] Jamal felt his British school, which was officially failing at the time, did not push him or develop his talent. In a BBC radio interview, the adult Jamal said:

> I think that attitude, that mentality to study hard and work hard was always frowned upon. The content of the Generating Genius programme was very challenging. We didn't just get to Jamaica to have a holiday. When we arrived, we went straight to the University of the West Indies. I later had the confidence and the knowledge to give a lecture about malaria, I was only 12 years old. The programme really stretched us intellectually. When I returned to Britain, I did have the experience of seeing black scientists and leaders, I saw a successful end game.[10]

The presenter Dotun Adebayo put a rhetorical question to the listeners, saying that Jamal seemed so focussed that he wondered whether he might have reached his goals without the help of Generating Genius. Were we just rewarding those who were going to make it anyway? But Jamal attended a school that was in special measures, at risk of closing. Teachers were leaving weekly. There were high exclusions of black boys, and few were able to attain the average standard of five GCSEs. Jamal was in danger of failure. He had no critical mass of support: we provided that framework for him to succeed.

I never tried to convert the boys to my perspective on race and politics. Despite the nature of our programme, I don't remember us ever discussing the subject. Was I being naive? Was I ignoring the realities of racism? I don't think so. I wanted them to feel the cool breeze of freedom, to understand that one of the biggest dangers wasn't racism, but shrinking their horizons, telling themselves they were trapped by white privilege. I wanted to focus on the positives, not the negative. We nurtured their talent and they blossomed. One of the Generating Genius alumni, Simeon Balson Jones, was the only state school student studying Physics at Imperial College, London at the time of the programme. He has a sophisticated understanding of the role of race in education:

> It's not necessarily race but more of an environment. If you send someone to Eton College, he is more than likely going to get into a top university. Compared to an inner-city state school, it's going to be a lot harder. I think your friendship group is key. I was talking to a group of friends at university, and it suddenly turned out that I was the only one from a state school.

Asked whether he felt that the curriculum could be more oriented to the interests of black boys, Simeon conceded that it could be better linked to wider interests, but came out with a fascinating line: 'But I think you should play the hand you are dealt with.'

Since leaving university, Simeon has been playing with a royal flush. He has never been out of work, signing up to some of the world's best corporates who are thankful for his software skills. He has also given back to Generating Genius, running coding camps and inspiring a new generation on the road to great careers.

School reports are always scattered with the cliché 'has potential' – as a teacher, I used it as a nice way of saying 'This student is bone idle'. But the truth is, everyone has potential; what I wanted to promote through Generating Genius was the right attitude.

It seems to me that there is substance to the criticism that we cherry-picked the boys most likely to succeed. However, it was the support we gave that was important in helping boys who might have fallen off the straight and narrow. We were under no illusions that we could solve the wider problem of a particular kind of black underachievement that had its roots in family breakdown and broader cultural issues. Nevertheless, the act of spotting talent and developing students in tough circumstances has great value. Some described us as the 'sharp middle-class elbows' that ensured a group of young people were able to realise their potential.

For 19 years, Generating Genius focussed on black African and Caribbean students. Early on, it moved from boys only to mixed sex in response to demand. Later, we realised that the educational landscape was changing. When we first started, we were focussed on London. However, as the educational outcomes of Londoners began to improve, it was the performance of young people outside London that worried us. It was also clear that working-class white students were significantly underperforming.

According to Paul Johnson of the Institute of Fiscal Studies:

> The educational success of nearly all ethnic minority groups is striking. A larger proportion of most achieve good GCSEs than do whites, despite being poorer on average. Among the poorest pupils – those eligible for free school meals – between 10 per cent and 30 per cent more children of Pakistani, Bangladeshi, black African and Indian heritage achieve five good GCSEs, including English and Maths, than do the poorest whites.[11]

This was supported by Oxford academic Steve Strand in his evidence for the Commission for Race and Ethnic Disparities. Key findings from his research are:

- White British and Black Caribbean students, both boys and girls, from low socio-economic status (SES) backgrounds are the lowest achieving groups of all students.
- Boys with low SES from Pakistani, White Other and Any Other ethnic backgrounds score below the average, but still score significantly higher than White British and Black Caribbean boys from low SES backgrounds.
- At middle SES, it is only White British and Black Caribbean boys who score substantially below the average.
- The achievements of Black Caribbean and Mixed White and Black Caribbean students more closely match that of White British students, particularly at low SES, than they match other ethnic minority groups.

American academics have been bolder when comparing the outcomes of African-Americans with those of different black immigrant groups. Ironically, they cite Caribbean achievement in America as an example of success. The picture in Britain is, of course, the opposite. However, there are lessons. We can look at the achievement of more recent immigrants to Britain such as the West Africans, who have an exceptionally strong belief in education as a way out of poverty. There is a real sense that 'immigrant optimism' is often a force that drives students through the education system.[12]

The change in the educational landscape did not surprise me because we always followed the data. We had identified early on that geography was significant: outside London, achievement was generally lower. In its first 15 years, Generating Genius had many successes in supporting students from London and the South East. We had a great programme, and it was high time to share this with the rest of the country and with the majority low-income white group, who were underachieving at critical levels.

In 2020 Generating Genius began to support students in other locations, such as the North East, North West, East Midlands and West Midlands, areas where there are fewer charities and opportunities for young people from deprived backgrounds. Expanding to support more students from these regions is a strategic priority for Generating Genius over the coming years. The charity still has a mission to support black London-based students, but its model can be adapted to reach all low-income students (including white working-class students) who have a passion for Science, Technology, Engineering and Maths. We will continue to support students to help them get into good universities, top companies and brilliant apprenticeships.

MAPPING OUT OUR FUTURE

We all need a map that shows us where to go. A map helps us to chart a course to our best times, and tells us we can use our optimism and agency to get there. If we have a sense of where we're going, it becomes easier to start putting one foot in front of the other. A map is about the future: it looks towards new destinations.

To continue with our map analogy, the Generating Genius programme also tries to keep us on the main roads. Just as we found in Hackney, going too specialist isn't the easiest route. Special race initiatives just don't always work. When we focussed on the main issues of good leadership, high expectations and subject knowledge, black children really succeeded. The idea that teachers needed lessons in unconscious bias training, or that black students needed sessions on how Egypt was a black kingdom, were nothing but big diversions.

Most of my own confidence and optimism I attribute to my mother and Jamaica. It was through her often idiosyncratic nurturing, which was far from perfect, that I learnt how to be free. My mother was fearless and yet vulnerable, which makes her truly human. For her, there was no tension in being very aware of the realities of racism and yet having the agency to get what she really wanted. She would have had little time for notions of 'imposter syndrome' or white privilege. In her workplace, where she was the only black woman among 20 white men, she – as they say in Jamaica – 'run tings'. I remember when my cousin was looking for a job and he asked her for help. The next day my five-foot-two mother went to the boss of her electronics component factory and asked him to employ my cousin in the warehouse. He explained to her that there were no vacancies, and the firm couldn't afford the hire. My mother's response was 'He starts on Monday'. The manager knew not to make her upset, and so my cousin got a job and moved up through the ranks.

You may say that not everyone has that level of confidence, and that they would struggle with a really nasty boss. I agree. However, my mother never underplayed her own agency. This power within may well need some nurture, nudging and navigation. But it characterises black success from early migration to the young scientists at Generating Genius.

When looking to intervene, then, we need to think of Jamaican sprinters. We need deeds, not words. And we need a plan. The six behaviours that we instilled with Generating Genius *worked*.

1. Teach the technique.
2. Set standards high and focus on core knowledge.
3. Be prepared to lose in order to win.
4. Repeat until it's effortless.
5. Give support and investment over the long term.
6. Be a father figure.

This is a road map for all black success. The proof? Jamal. Simeon. Wasseem. The proof is in those fantastic young people who are now out in the world doing great things. Just like Usain Bolt, they weren't born winners. They were made.

PART 2

BLACK SUCCESS

5

NIGERIA'S SCRABBLE FOR BRITAIN
THE REVERSE MISSIONARIES

I N the second part of this book, we will step away from my direct experiences and our earlier focus on education to talk more widely about black success. Among other things, we will look at the superlative results of West African Brits, the way in which narratives get twisted to fit agendas, and the peerless example of the Windrush Generation.

In each case, we'll be uncovering a surprising story of black success that cuts against the grain. Each story is instructive and inspirational, showing how real people have applied the principles that made Generating Genius such a success, and – more importantly – used their own agency to change their circumstances and their world.

Black success is too often considered a kind of sideshow, or something that is in some way 'alternative'. In this and the following chapters, I'm going to show that the contrary is true: that black success is actually at the heart of life in Britain today.

SCRABBLING FOR SUCCESS

For most of 2015 Nigeria was buzzing with excitement. The nation was ahead of China, America, Singapore, Russia and Great Britain. There was even talk of declaring a national holiday. Nigeria was a world superpower and it had just won the world championship.

At Scrabble.

Wellington Jighere became a Nigerian national hero, and a global superstar.[1] Children would sing his name. In the 2020s Nigeria still ranks as the top nation at Scrabble and for many the game is an obsession. But what does this all mean? Dig deep and we will find that it is about much more than just obscure words being lined up on tiles.

There are lots of things that make Nigeria's dominance in Scrabble improbable. First, language: for many players English is not their first tongue. Nigeria has over 500 languages spread out across its vast territory. Next, the game is imported and culturally associated with the English middle classes. Yet Nigerians feel no cultural oppression: playing Scrabble to them is as natural as eating jollof rice and listening to Afrobeat.

So how did it come about that a country with a reputation for corruption, kidnapping, poor governance and an impoverished underclass should become world champions at a mid-twentieth-century parlour game?

Two reasons. The short-word strategy. And *Naja no dey carry last.*

Let's take them by turns. Firstly, the strategy of playing mainly short words. It was not, at first, a no-brainer. But as I've shown repeatedly in this book, what we often find when we unpack black success is a perceived disadvantage being transformed into an advantage. Behind Jighere's affable manner was a calculating strategic mind, one that had grasped a key principle of Scrabbling success.

Jighere was puzzled at the way the rest of the world played Scrabble. The game combines language skills with strategy and competition. As words are placed on the game board, points are collected. Each letter has a different point value, and different squares on the board offer bonuses. The sum of the points for each letter, plus any bonuses, makes up the total number of points gained from spelling out any particular word. The most obvious strategy, therefore, is to play those words that have the highest score, and in practice that means longer words with rarer letters – X, for instance, rather than A. The rest of the world, in their desire for a quick win, pursued these long-word combinations. But what if this strategy had a hidden weakness?

Given that English is not their mother tongue, you would expect Nigerians to be at a disadvantage. They are the David up against the Goliath of English and its vast vocabulary. However, writer Malcolm Gladwell writes of how, in the Biblical story, the giant's strength becomes his weakness and David's weakness becomes his strength:

> He [David] runs toward Goliath, because without armour he has speed and manoeuvrability. He puts a rock into his sling, and whips it around and around, faster, and faster at six or seven revolutions per second, aiming his projectile at Goliath's forehead – the giant's only point of vulnerability. Eitan Hirsch, a ballistics expert with Israeli Defence Forces, recently did a series of calculations showing that a typical-size stone hurled by an expert slinger at a distance of thirty-five metres would have hit Goliath's head with a velocity of thirty-four metres

per second – more than enough to penetrate his skull and render him unconscious or dead. In terms of stopping power, that is the equivalent to a fair-size modern handgun. 'We find,' Hirsch writes, 'that David could have slung and hit Goliath in little more than one second – a time so brief that Goliath would not have been able to protect himself and during which he would be stationary for all practical purposes.'[2]

Just like Goliath, the Nigerians' opponents were carrying too much armour. They thought they were going into combat on their terms, but Nigeria came up with a game-changer. It was not the battle they expected, and the result left them, literally, lost for words.

'Short words are best, and old words when short are best of all,' said Winston Churchill. This is true when it comes to oratory: the best words are short and punchy. In Scrabble, the Nigerians used short words because they were easier to learn.[3] The short-word tactic had the added benefit of 'choking' the board, so the opponent had nowhere to go with their fat, long, flabby words. It is a kind of defensive play which throws opponents.

I find it strange when my more left-wing friends talk about Africa before the Europeans came as if it was some sort of socialist paradise, full of the milk of human kindness. Even today, lazy stereotypes tend towards depictions of Africans as peaceable, smiley folk living a simpler life. I'm (not) very sorry to burst this bubble, but what dominates the human psyche in Africa, as it does everywhere else, is competition. The instinct for competition, according to Nigerian travel journalist Rosie Bell, is everywhere. In an article for the BBC travel website, she wrote:

In a lifetime of feverishly competitive Scrabble-playing, I had only been defeated by six earthly beings. Growing up, my mother's nickname for me was 'Speedometer', and I began teaching myself German at the age of nine to catch up to the 10 languages my parents spoke between them. For Nigerians like me, a competitive streak is as natural as spicy jollof rice at a wedding.[4]

Out of the last five World English Scrabble Players Association Championships, a Nigerian has won three. There is a saying in Nigeria: *Naja no dey carry last.* It means Nigeria never comes last. Here, then, is the second reason for their success. Nigerians aren't messing around when it comes to Scrabble – they're playing to win.

As in Scrabble, so in life. Competition and aspiration are powerful drivers of excellence in Nigeria. The nation already has a long list of global achievers, and with the rise of 'Nollywood' – like Bollywood before it – looks poised for even bigger success. Some points on the roll call of achievement:

- Chimamanda Ngozi Adichie is a multi-award-winning writer.
- Afrobeat has become a musical phenomenon in nightclubs across the planet, from Jamaica to Japan.
- According to a 2017 US Census Bureau report on sub-Saharan Africans living in America, about 61% of people with Nigerian ancestry aged 25 and older had a first or higher degree – more than twice the US rate of 28.5%.
- Nollywood, Nigeria's film industry, is now the second largest in the world, and was valued at $6.4 billion in 2022.

Add Scrabble to that list. It's played everywhere, and the government has declared it to be a sport, not just a board game. There is a Nigerian Scrabble Federation, and it comes under the Ministry of Sports.

According to Rosie Bell:

So, what's behind this 'Nigeria never comes last' mindset? Lofty expectations are bestowed upon Nigerian children from an early age. We are taught to marry well, amass multiple degrees and earn enough to take care of our parents in old age. The firstborn carries the brunt of these expectations and should ideally support younger siblings, too. There are plentiful warnings against 'non-traditional' careers in the arts in favour of profitable vocations that offer respectable titles like doctor, barrister or engineer ... At the heart of this boundless aspiration is the fact that Nigerians place great value on being respected; they are tenacious, hard-working, status-driven and competitive. With more than 195 million Nigerians to contend with, a roll-up-your-sleeves mentality is certainly advantageous.

Rosie Bell also points to the optimistic, can-do mentality revealed in common Nigerian forenames: Godsfavour, Blessing, Godspeed and Goodluck (the name of the former president). This can be a bit intimidating for younger Nigerians, who have to live up to their name. In 2011 Nigeria was named the most optimistic nation in the world for the second year running. Cynics would argue that Nigerians at home contend with unbearable poverty and corruption, so that much of this optimism is misplaced. They will say that Nigeria may be in the race, but it is not among the winners. To an extent I agree. It would be naive to suggest that the ordinary Nigerian is living in some kind of utopia. But what I am pointing to is a spirit or mindset which – particularly when unleashed in America and Britain – is driving phenomenal success.

This chapter is about black success on a scale we simply haven't seen before.

ASPIRATION NATION

If Nigerians and Caribbeans have approached success differently, this should not be seen as some kind of divide-and-rule issue. The lessons for black British-based Caribbeans and African-Americans are, however, sobering. For too long we allowed a leadership that spoke of African roots and pan-African ties to pull off one of the biggest hustles in history. This leadership never really understood the complexity that is Africa and failed to acknowledge that Britain had changed. There was a time in our history when the pain caused by post-colonialist attitudes and rampant racism in Britain was a defining feature of our everyday lives. Africa was depicted as impoverished, wild and uncivilised, rather than the cradle of civilisation. It is right that we listened to orators and scholars who corrected this picture.

But where I believe we have gone wrong is in neglecting our own capacity to change our world. The race hustlers primed us to see Britain and America as spaces in which it was impossible for black people to prosper. The historic pain was turned into some kind of terminal psychological affliction. The result: our self-confidence has been totally sapped. Any black person who spoke of the opportunities that exist in Britain was called an Uncle Tom or a denier of racism.

Nigerians, though, have not drunk this Kool-Aid. Instead, they have used a spirit of aspiration and optimism to carry them through a newly opened door. It hasn't always been easy. The comedian Gina Yashere explains that there is a tension between the 'historic pain' and Nigerian optimism. I watched her on YouTube with great interest as she recalled how hard it was to succeed in Britain. Gina is proud of her Nigerian background. She grew up in Bethnal Green in the 1970s and speaks of having literally to run for her life from racist, knife-wielding skinheads. Even in the 'safety' of her school, she had to contend with abuse from black peers who derided her for being African. She puts this down to the fact that white supremacy made everyone feel it was open season on Africans.

I too can remember that time. In particular, I think of one occasion when I was 14 and we had just finished a cold-bitten football match in the local park in Penge. I was playing with a boy called Godfrey, who was a good friend and, like me, mad about football. I knew where he lived but had never met his family. Godfrey had left his gloves in the park, and I thought it would be a good deed to walk to his home and return them. He told us that he was born in Kingston, Jamaica and he came to England when he was five; he also said that his dad used to play football for Jamaica. In those days we always lied about our parents' professions. I used to say that my dad fixed rockets for NASA in America and he was now at home resting. I should have just said he was a car mechanic. When I rang the bell at Godfrey's house, a tall, elderly man answered the door. He was wearing the *abgaba*, a four-piece garment worn by Yoruba men. It consists of a large, loose-fitting outer dress (*awosoke*), an underwear jacket (*awotele*), drawstring trousers (*okoto*) and a traditional cap. My first thought was, 'This isn't very Jamaican.'

I said to the man: 'Is Godfrey in? I have come to return his gloves, he left them in the park.' The man replied: 'I can recognise my son's gloves … but who is Godfrey? Babatunde, come to the door, your friend is here.'

Babatunde, I said to myself. Godfrey is African.

Babatunde made me swear not to tell the others that he was Nigerian. In those days everyone wanted to be Jamaican. Being African was not cool. The likelihood is that, once outed, you would get a beating at school – and it would be the black boys doing the kicking. I found this paradoxical, perplexing and wrong. Here was my own Caribbean community jumping up and down about 'Back to Africa' and 'Africa for Africans' … yet many disliked the Nigerians who lived alongside them in Brixton.

According to Gina in her autobiography:

Nigerians are huge believers in reincarnation, and Mum has often told me that when she and her sisters were young, they'd often laugh as my grandmother regaled them with stories of who she would come back as in her next life. My grandmother had said she would return as the exact opposite of who she was, one of many wives of a Nigerian chief. She said she would return speaking perfect English, unfettered by any man, unburdened by children; she was going to see the world, work a man's job if she wanted and be a much freer spirit, doing whatever she wanted. Sound familiar?[5]

Gina is spiritual, and mentions how she was called 'Granny' by members of her family, in allusion to this kind of reincarnation.

She even has a birthmark on her neck that links her to her grandmother, who was scarred after an operation. As a young woman she became an engineer and worked for the lift company Otis as their first female engineer. They made her the poster girl of the company, appearing in brochures and marketing materials. But she faced terrible racism from her co-workers. They put banana skins in the pockets of her jumpsuit and pictures of monkeys on her desk. When asked if Britain has changed since those bitter days of the 1970s, she is adamant that it hasn't: for her racism has just gone underground.

The irony is that it is her own once despised Nigerian community that is now flying ahead in modern Britain. They are top achievers in education, university admissions, jobs in the City of London, and in the highest levels of government. This is a world that no one could have imagined in the 1970s. One of the key strengths of today's Nigerians in Britain and America is that they know how to be free.

As Britain and other Western powers reassess their history of colonialism, it is interesting to me that demands for reparations and apologies come from black people in the diaspora, rather than from Africans themselves. In an article for *UnHerd*, Nigerian academic Dr Remi Adekoya says:

> The general stance of Africans who live in Africa is certainly not to blame the former colonists for the problems of their countries today. They place the blame squarely on their ruling elites of a cursory glance of a newspaper in any African country will evidence. A majority – 59% – of Africans aged 18–24 believe that the impact their country's former colonial powers have on their education systems is positive, while a quarter (25%) disagree. A majority – 57% – also feel trade relations

with the former colonial power have a positive impact, while 27% disagree. Surprisingly for me, 47% even think the former colonial power's impact on their country's culture and identity is positive and 46% think their access to its natural resources has a positive effect, compared with 32% and 36% who disagree respectively ... These figures suggest the majority of African youths who actually live in Africa have quite different views from those in the West who are attempting to speak on their behalf.[6]

It's not that those 'back home' have uncritically accepted the colonial influence – there are abundant obvious negative legacies. But they have been free to creatively 'mix and blend' the world around them. So strong is their own culture that Nigerians have characteristically had the confidence to take the best aspects of other cultures and blend them into it. Christianity is a good example. It is not rejected as some 'outsider' Western belief; instead, Nigerians have taken it and run with it. They've woven Christianity into traditional folk religions, and these folk beliefs have become part of their Christianity. This is not shame or inferiority but a crafty art, a defensive play – what anthropologists call 'resistance within accommodation'.

With self-confidence comes the awareness that there are no bogeymen to blame, whether in history or current international politics. And the result is that power returns to you in the present day – if you see your government messing things up and being corrupt, you can challenge them without throwing up your hands and saying, 'This is inevitable.' That's the power of agency. It makes you believe that you are the author of your own life, and that you can change the world.

In Nigeria, then, Scrabble has become more than a game, more even than a competitive sport. It is a microcosm for the country itself. The short-word strategy is writ large in Nigerian culture. There is no idea here that the deck is stacked, or that success is a 'white man's game'. Scrabble is Scrabble – a game to win – and Nigerians are world-beaters.

THE PROSPERITY GOSPEL

On any given Sunday, at least half of all churchgoers in inner London are black, of African or Caribbean heritage, although this group accounts for only 13% of the capital's population. Some 240 black-majority churches in the South London borough of Southwark, almost half of them in one postcode, operate out of old bingo parlours, movie theatres, warehouses, and storefronts, among kebab shops and convenience stores. 'We suspect that this represents the greatest concentration of African Christianity in the world outside of Africa,' concluded social theologian Andrew Rogers.[7]

The Reverend Israel Olofinjana came to the UK from Nigeria in 2004. He acknowledges that there may be something positive about growing up in a country where there is more cultural commonality than there is in multicultural Britain. Is he saying that he had a slight advantage compared to black Brits like me, who were born here? Because I think there is something in that theory. When you are the majority, there is more of a foundation for confidence. Nigerian immigrants are not so tied to the specific racial and political history of the UK; they don't carry as much, or at least not the same, historic baggage. Also, when you arrive here from somewhere else, the opportunities for a better life are more salient than if you were born here. Olofinjana is talking about a sense of 'immigrant optimism' – an attitude that we more often associate with America. He admits that he is on a learning curve in his attempts to empathise with 'the Caribbean burden', to understand some of our challenges.

His optimism was energised by his church upbringing. He comes from a Nigerian Pentecostal tradition known as the 'Prosperity Gospel', which he says leads to empowerment. As with any religious sect, one needs to be on one's guard for flaws that could lead to the congregation getting exploited. However, I really like this version of Christianity. Imagine going to church every Sunday and being told that you can do and be anything you want in the world. This is 'agency' on full throttle – agency as a kind of spiritual mission.

Israel says:

> There is a version of Christianity which is about black agency – even though the pastors didn't use this term ... They will call it success, they will call it victory. They will speak about being a champion, being a conqueror. It is also practical, for it speaks to being successful in your education and career. I remember attending lots of seminars put on by my church telling us how to be successful in business or even marriage. All of this is imbibed. So, coming to the UK, I now see some Nigerian churches continuing with this message.

Most successful Nigerians are from the south of the country and are influenced by the post-colonial legacy of the British – hence Scrabble. This has helped them to find success in both the UK and America. They have a link to British culture, a degree of cultural understanding, which they can use when they arrive in a country less structurally racist than it was for migrants from the Caribbean. I'm not saying that people from the Caribbean had less of an understanding of British culture when they arrived here. They found a country that was familiar to them in certain regards, but they simply faced a more hostile environment than new arrivals today. What is rich about my dialogue with Israel is that he gets the complexities. He understands how Caribbean people might feel that Christians like him are missing the reality of lived racism. However, he also knows that success is driven by optimism.

I think everyone can learn from the Prosperity Gospel of the Nigerians – not because it is soft on racism, but because it creates an incredible mindset. It gives us the confidence to overcome class and race barriers. The idea that doing so loads structural problems onto the victim is a false premise. The truth is, we must fight both sides. We must make demands on institutions and people to change. But we must also be able to fight the battle within our heads – to fight against the part of us that finds it hard to accept that the landscape has significantly improved, to fight against the part that says our success is out of our hands. The Nigerians are building their own capacities, not compromising their culture.

In 2002 Britain initiated the Highly Skilled Migrant Programme to source top foreign talent into Britain. It was a way for employers to find talent without having to deal with the bureaucracy of work permits. To qualify, you had to show evidence of relative high income in your home country. Nigerians were ideally suited for this new scheme, as the country had a large supply of talented, educated middle-class workers in the big cities. Put simply, Britain scooped up a ready-made black middle class who wanted to escape Nigeria's relatively limited prospects. London offered affordable education and a better standard of living. Prior to this, most Nigerians coming to England worked low-level jobs while studying part-time to accelerate their social mobility; the new scheme offered a more direct route to the top jobs and professions. It also coincided with the high point of financial services, which were booming in Britain before the crash. If you had a high-level bank job in Nigeria, you could get an almost equivalent job in Britain at a far higher salary.

Finance guru Feyi Fawehinmi came to Britain in 2004:

> I worked briefly for an accountancy firm in Wimbledon and within nine months I got a job with the top firm JP Morgan. My salary doubled what I was earning as an accountant. This was commonplace amongst my Nigerian peers. We boomed in the financial boom.
>
> Financial services was incredibly diverse, right up to senior management. When I worked at HSBC, I only saw one guy who was white British. There were Nigerians, Zimbabweans, my manager was from Hong Kong. It was a very egalitarian space and pay was good.

Talking about his engagement with Britain, Feyi says he was lucky to meet people from his own country who had a positive perspective on living in London. It was when he met Kemi Badenoch, the international trade secretary whose parents were Nigerian, that he felt he had found a true kindred spirit: she, like him, loved Britain and said so openly. The Nigerians he met earlier may have felt this, but if so they kept it to themselves.

On the question of marriage and family life, he says:

The Nigerian church is a great socialising space, where most people meet their partners. I met my wife in the church. The authority of adults is a great source of power, which can be abused. However, it has been the framework that has kept our children focussed on education and fortified against peer group pressure. Nigerians have increasingly had to accept that their children who are here are British, and they should be proud of that; they don't want them stranded between two countries. The successful British child of African origin is British first, with a knowledge of Nigerian culture and practices. That's the successful model.

I asked him about the boldness with which Nigerians have settled in majority white neighbourhoods. He said that many Nigerians are at best indifferent to local histories. They will look at an area for its affordability rather than its reputation. It has been a great story of immigrant-led renewal, because their arrival has improved school results and prevented the closure of many church buildings, left empty by a local population that has other things to do on a Sunday.

The story of Nigerian success is underpinned by religious strength. In England and Wales, for the first time, less than half of the population now describe themselves as 'Christian'. This marks a sharp decline in Christian identification over the last two decades. In the 2001 Census a comfortable majority – 71.7% – identified as Christian. This dropped to under six in ten – 59.3% – in the 2011 Census, with the latest edition showing a further fall to 46.2%.[8]

What does this tell us about the state of Britain? At face

value, you would have to conclude that the majority of white British have given up on church. It could be said that England and Wales is now a 'minority Christian' country.

But the Nigerian population in South London is undertaking a revival of Christianity that is restoring the faith to our cities. Religion comes with some serious added value, particularly when it comes to strengthening institutions like marriage and encouraging high aspiration in areas like education. The Bible talks about the faithful being the 'salt of the earth', people who challenge the moral decay around them. But the term has a double meaning, because we also use 'salt of the earth' to mean ordinary people with no airs and graces. It is interesting how Nigerians have combined a wonderful down-to-earth honesty with a spirituality that is literally reviving the dying High Streets of London. According to social critic Rakib Ehsan, their presence has the effect of challenging mainstream modern values – and ironically this may mean restoring to Britain many of the values it has lost.

> One thing is for certain: socially conservative migrants, including those who are Christian, cannot be expected to 'culturally assimilate' into mainstreamed forms of moral decay. The revival of Christianity in Britain is reliant on ethnic-minority traditionalists living in inner-city areas and urban towns who are quite rightly resisting 'assimilation' into the hyper-liberal, secularised and materialistic mainstream.[9]

Nigerian academic Dr Remi Adekoya says:

> When we talk about successful Nigerians, we are talking about those from southern Nigeria, who are predominantly

Christians. 95 percent. That part was influenced by missionaries during the colonial period. Western education became a positive.

It left Nigeria divided, with a higher level of the southern part of the country getting a secondary and university education. That package of the acceptance of Christianity with western education had a major driving force in success today. You have to get a good education, work hard and aspire. That's why West Africans as a whole do well in the British education system. The parents are not joking, they make sure you have completed your homework.

Like others, Remi points to Nigerian family structure as the bedrock for success. This is linked to religion: it is a culture in which divorce is frowned upon, and people will stay together rather than break up. Although he acknowledges that this may not always be the best philosophy, it means the Nigerian community in Britain is based on a stable family unit. Beyond this, Nigerian success is driven by middle-class aspiration: they realise that their children can get a better life in London than in Lagos. They value the security, schools and stimulation that come from living in a developed country. Most Nigerians will not run Britain down, because they see the country as providing opportunities for black people that are unavailable in most countries around the world.

RICHES TO RICHES

There are key points of difference in the story of Nigerian success in the UK and in America. But there is also an important point in common: in neither case are these people desperate migrants with no capital searching for a better life. Many accomplished their good life in Nigeria – they just wanted an even better one for their children abroad. Too much discourse around black success has focussed on the rags-to-riches model. What we see with West African migration is a new story of expertise – ready-made talent being transported to New York and London.

A number of questions arise from this. Firstly, is it good for Nigeria if their affluent, educated elite leave their own country and come to Britain? Doesn't it represent something of a brain and capital drain that will make things harder for Nigeria? Secondly, if we are importing the Nigerian elite, often the super-rich, then aren't we just moving around already successful, privileged people? Their 'black success' is actually a function of class. It's worth thinking about, but what's clear in the data is that the Nigerian group in Britain is not a single homogeneous class. It is socially mixed, and both rich and poor share an optimism that Britain provides a space in which they can fulfil their aspirations.

Examples of driven Nigerian success are everywhere. Tokini Peterside – Nigerian-born but educated at Cheltenham Ladies College – founded ART X Lagos, a collective focussed on promoting African art worldwide. In 2016 she organised the first international art fair in West Africa. The current African art market is estimated to be worth over £11 billion. I love the way she took the indigenous art of her homeland and conquered the West.[10]

Education is another driving force. Dr Dayo Olukoshi is the headteacher of Brampton Manor Academy, a state school in East Ham in East London. The neighbourhood is poor, with many challenges, but the school has racked up a rich accumulation of successes. In 2018, it produced the best A level results in the country. One year, it sent more students to Oxford and Cambridge than Eton.[11]

Another rising star from a Nigerian background is the aforementioned Conservative MP Kemi Badenoch, who at the time of writing is minister for international trade. What drove Kemi to centre stage was her 2022 bid to become prime minister. It was a bold move, and she surprised everyone by making it into the final selection of four candidates and winning the backing of 59 MPs. This was nearly one in six of the parliamentary party, and included big hitters like Michael Gove.

Kemi is the MP for Saffron Walden, a beautiful market town with medieval origins in the heart of Essex. Its population is 90% white and only 0.8% black. This 'true blue' Conservative constituency has taken Kemi to its heart: she is a popular and respected MP, returned by huge majorities in recent elections. During the leadership election, there were polls of the Tory membership, which disproportionately hails from well-heeled rural heartlands, suggesting that had she been on the final ballot, she would have become the next prime minister: they simply loved her Nigerian/British Conservative values.

I will show my colours and say that I owe a lot to Kemi. She was the sponsoring minister responsible for taking forward the findings of the Sewell Report. What emerged from the Report were some wonderful 'Nigerian success traits', and it was largely owing to Kemi that we were able to get our recommendations safely into government policy. What Kemi did was focus on the content of the Report, rather than the way in which it was represented: she reminded our critics, both in parliament and in the media, that we never denied the existence of institutional racism – but that the evidence in the areas we looked at supported a more complex rationale for race disparity. She was fantastic in the chamber, batting away all the critics.

Kemi was and is no racism denier. She speaks of her real experience of racism and how she has had to fight it; but the sting is that she also speaks of how much she loves the UK. Kemi has her feet firmly on the ground and an astute understanding of how Westminster works. Born in Wimbledon to Nigerian parents, she spent parts of her early life in both the US and Nigeria. She now shows all the skills of a great Scrabble player: confident in contest as she takes on the media and the political opposition but also calculating, able to play both short and long words when needed. It isn't surprising that a British person, from a Nigerian background, has commentators seriously predicting that she will one day become prime minister.

As someone from a Caribbean background, I am happy to see that Nigerian (West African) immigrants have found an easier path to success than previous generations. This is not to say that one group is better than the other, but that the stories and contexts are clearly different. Yes, racism persists, but Nigerians have built a capacity that is transforming the social landscape of Britain. The irony is that colonial Christianity has been part of this success. The Prosperity Gospel, a wonderful mixture of hardcore conservative Christianity and good capitalist business management, has turbocharged a success ethos.

This isn't a community still struggling with the past – it is one driven by the present and the future. No one can dare accuse Nigerians of selling out or being conned by white Christianity. The version of Judaeo-Christian values that they bring was made in Africa by Africans. They reimagined their own Yoruba and Ibo cultures into the Christianity that was imposed by Europeans. They have now arrived on the shores of their former colonial dictators, ready to bring the lost back to Jesus. Nigerians are spearheading the concept of 'reverse' missionaries.

The great joys of Africa are only a bus ride away, in Peckham. In search of inspiration for black success? Look to the Scrabble players – worshipping a God in their own image and leading Britain to the Promised Land.

OEDIPUS REXPECT, OR HOW NIGERIANS ARE SOLVING THE OEDIPUS COMPLEX

You may well wonder. But firstly, a bit of background. While many of us think we know the story of Oedipus, and by extension all about the complex named after him, it's worth having a brief refresher. Oedipus was born to King Laius and Queen Jocasta of Thebes. However, a family curse said that he would kill his father and sleep with his mother. For this reason, he was abandoned on Mount Cithaeron nearby, with his ankles spiked together. Found by a shepherd, he was fostered by the King and Queen of Corinth. However, he ran away from home after being cursed by Apollo at Delphi, and 'innocently' killed someone in a brawl. Soon after, he relieved a plague-ridden Thebes by solving the riddle of the Sphinx – and was rewarded with the throne of the city and marriage to the widowed queen.

Oedipus Rex, the great play by Sophocles, opens with Thebes again plague-ridden: the only hope, according to the prophet Tiresias, is to discover who killed the former king of the city, Laius.

The story tells us that the curse on Laius came about as follows. While visiting his friend Pelops, he fell in love with and abducted the latter's beautiful son Chrysippus. In punishment for this violation of hospitality, Apollo forbade Laius any children of his own, which he disobeyed by fathering Oedipus. For this blasphemy, Apollo cursed him: 'Your child will kill you'. As you've probably guessed, the man Oedipus killed in a brawl was his father Laius and the widow he married was his mother Jocasta. The prophecy has come full circle and we are invited to savour the bracing paradox of a famous leader assiduously conducting a vigorous investigation into a crime whose perpetrator turns out to be ... himself.

It's a stunning piece of dramatic irony, applauded by critics and audiences through the ages, beginning with Aristotle. But before we go further, we should ask – is Oedipus really so innocent? Are the gods really so whimsically cruel? Many have thought so, and have understood the play as an admonitory reminder of human powerlessness in the face of Lady Luck. But if that's all there is, it's not much more than a highbrow sick joke about the fickle finger of fate. The proper response would be: 'High time, then, to abolish Apollo and all the Olympians, and/or move elsewhere'.

Of course, there's much more to the story than this. The myth would not have persisted if it simply told us that luck can cut in two directions. Something unspeakable somehow connects us with Oedipus. Freud suggested that the story spoke to family dynamics more generally. He claimed that in Oedipus we see the male child's desire to, metaphorically, kill his father as the prime competitor for the affection and love of his mother. But I think this bleak reading isn't quite right either. So what *is* Oedipus all about?

The unlikely answer is found in the success stories of West African boys in the UK. They give us the best clue to this ancient mystery and why this strange but brilliant play still resonates. The story goes a long way to explaining why Nigerian boys do so much better at school than their African-Caribbean and low-income white male counterparts.

What's in a name? *Oedi–pous* means 'swollen foot' (*oideo* is to swell, be troubled) and this nickname, given by the shepherd to the babe with the spiked ankles, stays with him (along with the limp). 'Swollen Foot' is not propitious. Unlike 'Big Foot' – whose name suggests 'Big Man' and by implication a mighty warrior – 'Swollen Foot' implies disordered motion, a troubled relationship to the ground beneath your feet, and someone who is 'too big for his boots': someone puffed up, inflated. And since we know the swelling arose from a parental curse, we may suspect that all this bigness comes as a response to littleness.

Although Oedipus did not in fact suffer from the Oedipus complex (nor, in fact, did Freud say he did), his story is one of secret antagonisms within a dysfunctional family. Instead of wanting to kill Pa so he could stay forever with Ma, he vowed to disown both of them (that is, his supposed parents, the King and Queen of Crete); and because of Sophocles's brilliant plot, this vow looks more like a heroic response to cosmic injustice than filial ingratitude. He ran away from a troubled home, carrying – as runaways often do – a mixture of guilt and righteous indignation. Yet he found, again, as runaways often do, that the further he ran, the closer it brought him back to his real home. It is this reading, that you can't escape your past no matter how far you run from it, that is surely the most compelling. Certainly, it rings truer than the Freudian tale of a boy who hates his Pa because he can't let go of his Ma.

I see a reflection of this story in my own work with black boys. There, the teenage rebel – and we have all encountered him – declares through dress and body language, at least, that he has complaints against the culture. He is usually willing (eager!) to discuss these complaints, beginning with the many ways in which his parents have failed him. But there's a point of difference here. Oedipus betrays no sign of complaint, apart from that strange limp, and has apparently been the respected *tyrannos* of Thebes until the argument with Tiresias induces him to reveal that he thinks prophecy, Delphi, Apollo and indeed the whole of inherited culture are bunk – or at least only meaningful as the theatre in which his immense vanity can be gratified. Another reading could easily be that Oedipus needs to follow the rules of the culture, even when they seem unfair.

Teen boys will recognise all this. But it is particularly tough for black boys, who already feel that society is against them, to also face a family structure that demands obedience or faith even when that family has let you down. In modern terms, I am thinking of fathers who abandon their sons: a disproportionate reality in African-Caribbean families.

Anthropology tells us that the function of male initiation rites among developing peoples everywhere is to wean young lads from their mothers' skirts and 'blood' them into the warrior law of the fathers. That is to say, part of their purpose is to cauterise, repress and abolish excessive attachment to mothers and to vaccinate against rebellion towards fathers. This is frequently enacted as a leading of the child out of wild 'nature' and into 'culture'. Variations of such coming-of-age ceremonies are found in African, ancient Greek and Jewish culture. Bar mitzvah for boys at age 13 is the Jewish celebration of reaching adulthood. It means coming of age and taking on the full extent of the *mitzvot* – taking responsibility for your actions, present and future. It is a joyous occasion, the catalyst for a happy and fulfilling life as a Torah-observant Jew.

The richness and sophistication of Yoruba culture is quite wonderful. However, it is not only a source of ethnic pride. One function of culture everywhere is that it helps to prevent young men from tearing down the village. This is true in Persian, Roman and Greek cultures. Our ancestors had to inculcate a respect system that was hierarchical. Yoruba culture does this wonderfully well. An adult who is not a relation is often addressed as Uncle or Aunty. The body must also be used to signal that a young person knows their place. This may entail kneeling, touching the floor, or even full prostration in the presence of one's grandparents or in-laws. Elder respect is a renowned phenomenon in the Yoruba culture, and it is something Yoruba people take pride in. It is an important aspect of their tradition, passed down from each generation to the next as the source of a peace and orderliness considered sacrosanct in their daily life.

This issue of elder respect is not a matter of negotiation or choice. Respect is simply a given – it's not something an older person must earn. They have it as a consequence of their age. This is often hard for more Westernised cultures to understand. Here in Britain, teachers are taught to earn the respect of their students. But respect is a societal norm in Yoruba culture, which recognises that questioning it may well be a community's undoing. This does not mean that the culture is docile, or indifferent to abuse or racism on the part of elders. Rather, it's about child development and understanding the instinctual drive of young men towards war and sex. Rituals and orderly routines were designed to contain these dangerous urges.

Nigerians have been able to preserve these elder rites even when migrating to Britain and America. This has been a valuable source of resilience in cultures where fathers are often absent and the elderly are devalued. It has also given their young men a respect for the authority of teachers and the given hierarchy of schools.

The more a society succeeds in this, the less it will be troubled by transgressive desire. Conversely, as a society loses or changes direction, its hold on gender roles will become lax and confused, and transgressive desire will thrive. Athenian culture in the later fifth century BC was under considerable pressure for such a change in direction, which is to say that 'Oedipal' energies were on the rise: fathers and sons were in dispute, prophecy and the old religion were under attack, women were restive, complex sexualities, class-war activities and lawsuits for impiety (*asebeia*) were commonplace – all signs of deep instability. It's a picture we can recognise.

Could it be that too many black boys have been sent on the adolescent journey ill-equipped to complete the challenge? In the woods, they meet other boys left on their own, bitter with a world that has left them fatherless. They return to the community with their new adopted families. But now they are driven by a feeling of revenge against a world that gave them no maps, no torches, no loving memories, no sense of agency, no family. The initiation journey may be risky, but it should never be reckless. In our own African-Caribbean community, the data shows that over 60% of boys are raised in single-parent households. In Jamaica, it's an eye-watering 70%. Too many boys suffer a reckless initiation, and ask themselves why they were born with their ankles lashed together.

However, there is a happy story here, too. It's that many African communities understand that rites of passage are more than just a ceremony. They are built into the heart of a family structure, where the father is a key participant. I have noticed that many single black women from my own community understand this narrative both for boys and girls. They ensure, where they can, the involvement of fathers in the development of their children. If this is impossible, they do their best to 'father' their sons.

The skills displayed by Oedipus are detachment, cool thinking, objectivity, not letting one's judgement be swayed by fears or desires: these are the hallmarks of mathematics, medicine, deductive reasoning, the law courts and empirical science, all thriving in classical Athens. As the great classical scholar Bernard Knox has demonstrated, much of the play is given over to a demonstration of these skills by Oedipus, who 'investigates, examines, questions, infers ... knows, finds, reveals, makes clear'; and since these are the very skills of critical rationalism leading fifth-century Athens into a world of secular enlightenment, the intellectual virtues of Oedipus would have been readily perceived by his audience.

With all this scientific knowledge, Oedipus should be on his way to the Athenian equivalent of Oxford and Cambridge, before going on to a life as a leader and role model for his community. Unfortunately, conjoined to this is the disturbing fact that this new man, autodidact, son of chance, is not only the Tyrant of Thebes (the proper term for a self-made king who rules by usurpation, not birth), but actually tyrannical in nature. It's worth mentioning here that there has always been a sophistic argument that the rules of culture (*nomoi*) are conventional arrangements to be manipulated and exploited by those born strong enough by nature (*physei*) – as Oedipus clearly was. Does all this suggest that the new 'enlightened' mentality was somehow implicated in a 'tyrannous' loss of political virtue? Aristophanes certainly thought so, as did Plato.

How many black or white boys lose their temper with the teacher – or, worse, with each other? So many of our knife-crime statistics have come about as a sacrifice on the altar of being 'disrespected', or challenged on hearsay. This involves so much more than being oversensitive. Like Oedipus the Tyrant, these boys have lost an inherited identity and constructed a new one with their knowledge, intelligence and resourcefulness. But when the wind blows against this newly constructed identity, a rage is released. They have become the 'unparented', the 'son of chance'.

Oedipus does not dream of marrying his mother, as the Freudian skirt-clinger would, but, on the contrary, of neutralising her threat *by becoming unmothered*, incorporating her within himself and thus becoming *causa sui*: 'I intend to see the seed that gave me birth'. He will thereby acquire an annulment of the dependency he cannot help but feel. If mothers can be blanked, he is free to christen himself 'son of Tyche', goddess of Chance; which is to say, declare himself to be something random, spawned in a ditch (or found in the bulrushes). He will become less than human – or perhaps *more so*. In short, a cultural nothing who might thereby become an everything – an astonishing superman, a gift from the gods, and (in death) a focus for hero worship. Today, we need only look at those troubled rappers, deceased, who are still given props.

The struggle is on an intense level here in Britain, and, despite the strong Nigerian culture I valorise here, we increasingly open the papers and see African surnames attached to both the perpetrators and victims of knife crime. It is not just a Caribbean issue. Apollo is still vexed. At the same time, Nigerian families know that it takes a family to raise a child, and that this should never be left to chance.

6

NURSING THE WRONG IMAGE
THE CURIOUS JOURNEY OF MARY SEACOLE

I N the mid-1990s, black youths in the inner cities of America started a trend: they would make Bart Simpson black. In what can only be described as a phenomenon, Bart Simpson got a makeover. Soon everyone was wearing a black Bart Simpson T-shirt. He was given an assortment of black hairstyles and linked with rap stars.

Long before social media, Black Bart went viral. Instead of posts and Insta photos, kids were on the streets wearing newly styled trainers and tracksuits adorned with the Black Bart icon. One of the most memorable, to me, was a T-shirt of Nelson Mandela standing over Bart, who's saying, 'He's my hero'.

Harry Allen, music writer and avowed 'hip-hop activist', as well as a publicist for the rap group Public Enemy, said, 'I think the Bart character is appealing because – I don't want to say he's kind of black. I don't mean that. He's just got some very unusual characteristics, from his haircut to his use of the word "homeboy" infrequently, to even his general sassiness.' (In *The Simpsons*, Bart has also used the funky phrase 'work that body'.) Bedecked with gold chains and snazzy sneakers, Black Bart glares from another shirt that reads: 'You should understand' – a slogan playing on another Afrocentric T-shirt motto: 'It's a Black thing'.[1]

The trend spread to London and Birmingham, and for a while you saw black youths everywhere proudly sporting a black Bart Simpson T-shirt. I knew of one person who was making a lucrative business cashing in on the new fashion. Although it didn't last long, the speed with which the trend took off and grabbed the imagination was remarkable. There were spin-offs into cartoon sketches and street art. I loved this reverse appropriation. Black youth seemed to be saying that for years the media establishment had fed off their street culture in fashion, language, and style – and now they were going to do the same thing in reverse. It was, in some sense, cultural appropriation.

Appropriation of current and historic images has often been a great, playful way in which black people have reinserted themselves into popular culture. I think the Rastafarians are a great example. Their reimagination of white Christianity flipped the faith into a version that made sense to them. But where this reimagining loses the plot is when it tries too hard to make historic images 'blacker' than they really were. One example has been the Victorian entrepreneurial nurse, Mary Seacole. During the 1980s, in a passionate attempt to find great black role models to support the new multiculturalism, Mary was subject to a Bart Simpson-style makeover.

In 1805 Mary Jane Grant Seacole was born a 'free person' in Jamaica, the daughter of a white Scottish army officer and a black Jamaican landlady. Her profession was as a traditional herbalist, hotelier and general storekeeper. She was also a keen traveller, and her big break came when she went out to tend to British soldiers during the Crimean War.

It is Mary's encounter with Florence Nightingale that has turned this story into a racial punch-up of mythic proportions. The accepted story is that Seacole wrote to Miss Nightingale offering to help and share her nursing expertise, only to be rejected by Nightingale and the wider white establishment because she was black. The story then has Seacole bravely deciding to go out to the front on her own, so determined was she to help British soldiers. In this version, Florence Nightingale becomes the celebrated 'Lady of the Lamp', with the history books making her the founding mother of modern nursing – while Seacole is a forgotten heroine.

Great story. But unfortunately, the reality was more complex. According to Robert Dingwall, Seacole travelled to England in 1854 to make good on prior investments linked to gold-mining shares. Once she discovered that the shares were worthless, she came up with the idea of tending to the needs of soldiers fighting in the Crimean War, some of whom had been previously stationed in Jamaica. This was as much about commercial opportunism and entrepreneurial spirit as the selfless passion of a nurse who wanted to do good. There is evidence that she had offered to help in a nursing capacity, and was turned down. But there is no evidence that this was based on her race: more likely it was a lack of flexibility on the part of the British authorities, who found it hard to accommodate her unorthodox occupational history. It was after this rejection that Seacole set up her 'British Hotel', where officers could recover from their injuries and she could sell them her home-made remedies. According to Dingwall:

When there was a battle, she went off to sell wine and sand-
wiches to the spectators. It may seem odd today but battles at
this period were spectator sports – fashionable Washington
society drove out to watch the early battles of the American
Civil War, for example. After the battles she helped to search
for wounded or dying soldiers, occasionally with stray bullets
or shells flying around.[2]

After her death, Mary Seacole dropped off the radar for
decades. She had published an autobiography entitled *The
Wonderful Adventures of Mrs Seacole in Many Lands* in 1857: an
entertaining read, it was a bestseller at the time. To use the language of so-called branding consultants, she 'controlled her own
story'. Seacole would have had a wonderful time with today's
social media outlets – Facebook or Twitter. Unfortunately for
her, she had to rely on the humble book as her marketing tool –
but she knew that the best way to sell her healthcare products
was to package them up with her story.

The significance of the modern revival of Mary Seacole is
that, like Bart, she gets a makeover. The makeover has very
little to do with the real life of Mrs Seacole, and everything to
do with the racial politics of today. Young black people in the
1990s saw the power of reverse appropriation and were able to
disrupt a mainstream icon – Bart Simpson. However, similar
credit cannot be given to those who tried to reimagine Mary
Seacole after she was rediscovered in the 1980s and 1990s.
This was the era of town-hall multiculturalism, when Britain
was trying to rid itself of the nasty open racism of previous
decades. I've already described this era as one in which *The
Voice* newspaper was getting fat on local government adverts.
Schools were similarly eager to reflect a more diverse Britain.

None of this was really about scholarly attempts to unpack our past: it was about inclusion. The drawing of comparisons between Seacole and Nightingale is typical of the way in which we reconstruct history. In her book *Mary Seacole: The Making of the Myth* (2014), Professor Lynn McDonald points out how this culture war was stirred up in order for Seacole to get representation on a stamp (issued in 2006) and in a statue (eventually erected in 2015).

What really annoys me about this modern makeover is the way in which Seacole is depicted as some kind of Victorian Angela Davis. Children's books line her up next to the likes of Nanny of the Maroons and Michelle Obama. These books even give her a darker complexion, to hide her mixed heritage. Seacole is often rolled out for Black History Month as an example of the so-called strong black woman. She has become an icon, a paragon of virtue, a symbol.

But being a symbol has erased Seacole's ambivalent relationship with actual racial communities, such as her fellow Creoles (mixed race) or black Jamaicans. In her memoir, Seacole barely mentions her mother's side of the family, and nor does she bring up local politics around race, class, labour and rights. Seacole was from the small business-owning class of Jamaica, and her book is an attempt to sell a product. On the other hand, she was aware of racism, wondering whether the ladies of the Crimean War hiring committee rejected her because her 'blood flowed beneath a somewhat duskier skin than theirs'.

This is often quoted to show Mary Seacole's victimhood. But what I hear in Seacole's statement is *surprise* at the way she is being treated. She may now be a perennial heroine of Black History Month, but it is likely she had a very different conception of blackness to the one we have today. Seacole was never driven by black nationalism or anti-racism. She was driven by her own ambition. The surprising truth is that the status of 'successful black woman' has been foisted upon some-one who did not see herself in these terms. Her class and colour are important aspects of her story of courage, but it was her unique personality and determination that led her to transcend the obstacles she faced. My contention is that Mary Seacole saw herself as Mary Seacole first and foremost – an individual.

For me, her strength is the way she managed, as a woman in that time, to forge ahead with a business enterprise. However, she was no anti-colonialist. My sense is that Jamaica now adopts her in the spirit of its rather strange national motto: 'Out of many, one people'. The island is 97% African in origin and yet it indulges in notions of identifying as a multiracial society. The motto is also ironic because of the massive class divide that has persisted from Emancipation to the present.

An obituary written by her sister for the *Daily Gleaner* said of Mary: 'She was an old Jamaican character who was quite a notable figure in her day and who was representative of a class of Jamaican women which have almost wholly passed away.'[3] The quote reveals something of Jamaica's ambivalence about its past: it wants to give it a good kicking, but also can't seem to let it go. I have always found it amazing that Jamaican governments will wax lyrical about being independent, anti-colonial warriors, and yet have chosen to keep the jurisdiction of Britain's Privy Council. Put simply, the last judicial arbiter in a court case is not Jamaica's Supreme Court. It is left to a group of old white Englishmen to give the final judgment. Seacole is a similar figure: she's a symbol of radicalism, yet she is also a figure of colonial nostalgia. According to Robert Dingwall:

Mrs Seacole's memoir forms the main basis of her transformation into an icon of nursing since the 1980s. University buildings, scholarships and hospital wards have been named for her. Nursing textbooks celebrate her alongside Florence Nightingale; the study of her life and work has been inserted into the National Curriculum used in English high schools. Historic markers have been placed on buildings in London where she lived, and a statue has been erected. Her life has been featured in television programmes for a variety of audiences.[4]

She is a fantastic example of black success, and we should celebrate Mary Seacole as a black entrepreneur. For much of her life, until she became ill, she was a successful businesswoman and an adventurous traveller. There is no doubt that she was kind and generous. When she died, it seems as though most of the House of Lords came out for her funeral in London. She was buried in Kensal Green Cemetery, the same burial ground in which Jamaican national hero Marcus Garvey would initially be entombed. It was her business acumen, and her ability to network in high places, that made her a household name in Victorian upper-class circles. According to Dingwall:

> This case is, in some ways, the obverse of the present controversies over people like Cecil Rhodes and John Calhoun, where the complexities of the historical record are lost in conflicts about iconography. The contemporary universities and hospitals that have rushed to adopt Mary Seacole really should have had more respect for historical scholarship in attempting to address their own concerns about diversity. There are more genuine black heroines like Kofoworola Abeni Pratt (c.1910–1992), who is believed to have been the first

black nurse to work in the English National Health Service, was active in anti-colonial movements, and played a central role in the decolonization of Nigerian nursing. Too many people who ought to know better have preferred to print the legend rather than respect the evidence.[5]

Unfortunately, the pendulum is now swinging in the other direction. There has been a rush of studies seeking to undermine Mary Seacole and turn her into a fraud. What they miss is that her significant contribution was in business, not nursing. She has been given the wrong prize. She offers a remarkable template for success, using her Creole status as an opportunity. The irony for her modern cheerleaders is that it was all accomplished along the tramlines of Empire and global capitalism. The hero of today's Black History Month was really driven to Britain to check on her gold investments: this was no compassionate nurse wallowing in the mire with injured soldiers, desperately trying to patch up their wounds. She used what she had, and who she was, to build a successful business.

Presumably because the curators of black history tend to be affiliated with the left, they rarely focus on how Mary Seacole succeeded as a businesswoman. Their obsession with trying to wrestle her into a comparison with the white Florence Nightingale has given us a caricature version of Seacole. She is made fit for the needs of modern white guilt and black historic racial trauma. But we overlook the real story of her success – the real, inspirational, conflicted human being that she was.

Instead of trying to make Seacole into some kind of super-nurse, we need to understand her 'exceptional' status in colonial Jamaica. She was freer than poor black women and, ironically, freer in some senses than white women. She wasn't exposed to the overprotection that was afforded a respectable white woman, while on the other hand she had the credentials to get close to the white power base. This allowed her the freedom to travel and have adventures. Within this framework, she still needed to have courage, confidence and cash. This was not a woman who fought the Empire, but one who moved within its structures. She got going with what she cared about.

Seacole was a pioneer on the frontier of the New World, an entrepreneur in business and public health. With guile, a winning personality and useful contacts, she developed a fantastically successful international medical service. In the early part of her career, British soldiers, sailors and workers often went to her for alternative medicines as they tried to adjust to the Jamaican climate. Word got round that her medicines worked. She was running a boarding house and a tearoom while scaling up this alternative pharmacy. These men would soon offer a ready-made market for mobile privatised medical support. Mary Robinson, in her book *Mary Seacole*, says:

> She would attribute her success to instincts and acumen inherited from her mother, the fruits of it would be all the sweeter for being her birth right, courtesy of her father as an Imperial Briton …
>
> Here she was now, however, fifteen years a widow, preparing samples for the treatment of distinctly unlovely diseases, and managing the second-best hotel in slowly crumbling Kingston. She was learning more about Western medicine to complement the traditional knowledge her mother and her own experience gave her, but was astute enough to recognise that no matter how proficient a practitioner she became, it would lead so far in colonial Jamaica, and no further.[6]

It was this last point about the limitations of the local environment that drove her to look outward. This was equally true of my parents' generation and has driven the talent drain of Jamaicans right up to the present. In Seacole's day, not only were soldiers and sailors on the move, but labourers were needed for the new railway that would open in Panama. In 1848 gold was discovered in California and there was a corresponding rush across the world as people sought to get rich quick. Mary knew that if she set up near Panama, there would be a need for hotel and medical services for those making the journey to San Francisco.

The same spirit of adventure and enterprise led Mrs Seacole to the Crimea. In war, the reform of medical care was (literally) painfully slow. The chance that wounds would lead to death or life-changing injury was high. Two women helped to change this reality, but their histories and legacies have been doctored in the service of identity politics. This chapter is about that change, but also about how history is twisted to suit the agendas of the present – and what this tells us about success, agency and the importance of the stories we tell ourselves.

It was no secret that Florence Nightingale did not like Mary Seacole. She spread rumours that Mary was a quack with little medical skill who was really running a whorehouse for the soldiers. None of these accusations was true. Seacole had arrived on Florence's turf, and she obviously felt threatened. But this was no race war, and neither is it the case that one was necessarily better than the other – they were competitors but had very different skillsets. Mary Robinson sums up the rivalry and how it has been exaggerated to suit a modern-day discourse of race victimhood:

Mary Seacole could never be a model Nightingale nurse, even though she is often regarded as a black pioneer of the profession. She was a mixture of doctor and apothecary, surrogate deathbed mother (or even wife, on occasions), practitioner, comforter and – always – entrepreneur. She insisted on being useful to the sick and healthy, with, if possible, mutual profit both spiritual and material. Had she been successful in her interview in London in the autumn of 1854, and accepted as one of Florence's angels, she might possibly have managed for a while. But I very much doubt it: her skills and needs reached beyond what Florence sought … It does both women a disservice when modern commentators on the war compare Mary's medical skills with Florence's: they approached whom they wished to help quite differently, and relied on their own considerable but idiosyncratic gifts to try, with all their might, to treat patients with dignity and compassion.[7]

When Seacole was resurrected in the 1980s, those digging her up were on the left. Their mission was to rubbish Nightingale and enhance Seacole.[8] This culminated in the erection of a statue in London and a 2004 poll in which she was voted Britain's top Black Brit. But all this overlooks her greatest role: as an imaginative businesswoman.

INWARD REACH, OUTWARD STRETCH

Strong opinions, a sense of adventure, a flair for business, making contacts and marketing: all these qualities can be found in other examples of black success.

The poem 'Colonisation in Reverse' by Louise Bennett is about success. It starts with the words 'What a joyful news', as the speaker tells 'Miss Mattie' that Jamaica is colonising England in reverse. She says Jamaicans from all over the country and of all ages are leaving for England by the hundreds and thousands, and their plan is to get a good job and to settle in the new country. And if not jobs, then the dole isn't too bad. The people who do not like to travel are showing their loyalty to those who do by opening agencies that offer cheap fares to England. Therefore, week after week, large numbers of Jamaicans are finding their way to England. The speaker says that she finds this amusing, because now Jamaicans are the ones who are feeding off the English. There is a kind of ironic revenge. It's our time now. The task of the new independent Jamaica is *not* to go and help their old masters in Britain, who are in need after the war. The poem speaks to the idea that there is agency and choice. The key lines ask how the former coloniser will cope:

> Wat a devilment a Englan!
> Dem face war an brave de worse,
> But me wonderin how dem gwine stan
> Colonizin in reverse.[9]

This takeover will not be through guns, rape and pillage but through the soft power of culture. In the 1960s Bennett was pointing to what was then the new phenomenon of globalisation. Caribbean people in this period would use their colonial status as a Trojan horse to enter the mother country and change Britain – not destroy it – forever.

This idea has been articulated best by the Jamaican-born Harvard academic Orlando Patterson. In his book *The*

Confounding Island, he argues against the idea that industrialisation and modernisation lead to the standardisation of behaviours, cultures and consumption – to what is often called the 'McDonaldisation' of culture ('one size fits all'). Patterson says that Jamaica's engagement with the world offers a counter to this pessimistic view of modern capitalism. Here again, the colonised can be seen influencing the Western coloniser. Patterson illustrates this in the way that Jamaican music has impacted the world stage, starting in Britain. He says:

One other factor was equally important in explaining the rapid spread of reggae and its eventual emergence as a global music form. This was the large-scale migration of working-class Jamaicans. The first such movement was to Britain, where Jamaicans effectively transformed what had previously been an all-white country into a multiracial society. By 1964, a thinly Anglicised version of ska known as blue beat was already in vogue. In 1969 a song by Desmond Dekker from the previous year, 'Israelites', became the first reggae track to make it to number one on the British hit parade as well as the first to crack the top ten in the United States. Almost no one outside of Jamaica understood Dekker's Jamaican lyrics and therefore hadn't the slightest clue that they had been inspired by the Rastafarian theological view of black Jamaica as the 'true' Israelites suffering Babylonian exile in Jamaica and yearning for the day they would return to Zion. By the mid-1970s, Jamaican music had been completely embraced by white British youth, who by then viewed it as an integral part of their culture. (Davis and Simon (1979) 1992, Partridge 2010). From its British base, it would spread rapidly throughout continental Europe and north and sub-Saharan Africa.[10]

As the founder of Island Records, Chris Blackwell helped not only to mastermind Bob Marley's success, but also that of Grace Jones, U2 and Robert Palmer, to name but a few. Even though he was raised in Jamaica, his ancestry was a far cry from my own. A white boy whose family belonged to the plantocracy of Jamaica, he used his privilege and connections to bring Jamaican music to the world. What I find fascinating about his comfortable journey to the UK is how, in terms of mindset, his attitude and that of my parents' generation were aligned. Like them, he came to Britain as an entrepreneur, a buccaneer and a visionary. And what he did was tap into the strength of the Caribbean community that had quickly developed, particularly in London. In his memoir he says:

> I was constantly on the lookout for opportunities and alliances, checking what was happening in the clubs and pubs, seeking out those who could help me work out manufacturing and distribution. Once I had my bearings, I focused on the parts of London and England where Jamaicans were starting to create local communities. This was my initial target audience.[11]

Blackwell had a monthly stipend from his rich folks in Jamaica, which meant he was able to mix with the uptown Old Etonians when needed. Still, he was smart enough to do two things. First, he used the experience and skills he'd gained in Jamaica as a record producer. Second, he recognised that Jamaicans in London had buying power. In relation to the British music industry of the 1960s, he says:

> Britain was behind Jamaica in many ways, certainly in terms of how that intensification of influences was leading to a singular

local style and various new kinds of music, and in terms of how collaboration among artists, engineers, entrepreneurs and musicians, the sheer joy of discovery, was creating new sounds and a prolific new kind of business.[12]

Blackwell talks of coming across Jamaicans who were exploiting the new market, based as it was on a community hungry for music from back home. They remind me of our modern bedroom producers, using the internet to develop and share new music.

It is here that we see once again the Mary Seacole business model. Blackwell, like Seacole, has a restless spirit expressed in a need to travel. He recognises the limitations of his home market. He sells to the community he knows, follows them across the world and becomes a master at marketing his product to a wider audience. He, like Seacole, uses his class and race to make business networks and contacts. Blackwell, of course, is white – so how is this 'black success'? Because the result is that reggae music takes off internationally. Through Blackwell, Bob Marley becomes, to date, Jamaica's most successful export. I am not saying that Chris Blackwell studied Mary Seacole and then built his empire. But I am saying that both drew on the same business universals to achieve success. Blackwell's and Marley's legacy lives on. A recent study by money.co.uk revealed that if Marley were still alive he would be making an estimated $1,667,878 each year from streaming and social media.

The popularity of reggae was harnessed by entrepreneur Levi Roots when he made his pitch on the BBC TV show *Dragons' Den* in a bid to launch his Reggae Reggae Sauce business. I remember sitting back to watch the programme. I was about to change channels, bored with the first two prospects, when I saw Levi in his dreadlocks walking up the stairs with a guitar, singing this really catchy tune, 'Reggae Reggae Sauce'. When the 'dragons' saw him, they were almost wetting themselves with excitement. In a way, his pitch was awful as he was hopeless with the numbers; but he *did* know his product. Immediately, Dragon Peter Jones put his money down and Levi Roots and his sauce became household names. The song was a hit and Levi became a millionaire, with television, radio and book deals. It all shows the power of slick marketing and brand proliferation.

I was honoured to meet Levi, who told me that he was a reader of my column when I was at *The Voice*. I can't help but feel that he had plenty of business acumen in the Mary Seacole style. Mary was popular in military circles and, when times were hard, they supported her work. They became her mechanism to scale her products. For Levi Roots, Peter Jones and his network became the mechanism to scale the production and distribution of his product. Like Seacole, he created a product that wasn't just for black people, but for everyone. The sauce had already proved popular at the Notting Hill Carnival, but he wanted to break out of his audience and go worldwide. Like Seacole, he was fantastic at marketing himself and his product: no one will ever forget his musical entrance into the Dragons' Den. It meant that, unlike many of the other prospects that appear on the show, the Dragons didn't just invest in Levi's business, they also invested in the man himself. Levi was a walking and talking billboard for his brand. And he had the good sense to leverage affection and trust in another global brand: reggae music.

Another brilliant networker, who came straight out of the Mary Seacole playbook of entrepreneurship, was DJ Jazzie B.

During the 1980s he was one of my icons. He was doing something in Britain that was hopeful and positive, and drawing energy from an unexpected source. In terms of music, black Britain seemed still to be dominated by the sounds of Jamaica and America. Basically, nobody was taking the 'Black Brit' seriously. We needed to make a mark on the world, and we needed to punch harder culturally. Jazzie, who was born in London but of Caribbean heritage, says of his upbringing:

> I actually grew up in north London; Hornsey Rise, Finsbury Park is the area where I grew up. Hornsey was predominantly like, a lot of black people, a lot of Greek people, a lot of Asians as well, particularly, even if you look at it now, in Stroud Green Road and places like that, predominantly Asian and black. The school I went to was a similar mix of various different ethnic backgrounds, and we had a strong presence of a lot of black people, particularly from the Caribbean. I think it really lent a hand towards being able to understand different cultures, particularly London being that melting pot or sweltering pot, or whatever, and I think it helped to shape my life in the future as well.[13]

Here Jazzie B points not only to the key to his creative success but also to the factors that have made black Britain the centre of a new diaspora and a new sound. His parents, who came here from Antigua in the 1950s, wanted their cheeky-chappy son to be a doctor or lawyer. However, influenced by the culture of the Jamaican sound systems, he turned his engineering skills towards building a system and becoming a DJ. But this would not just be someone to spin the discs on a Saturday night at someone's 18th birthday party. Jazzie had a bigger vision for the role.

Enter the Tories' Enterprise Allowance Scheme. This initiative, which was set up by Margaret Thatcher in the early 1980s, gave a guaranteed income of £40 per week to unemployed people who set up their own business. The intended recipients were self-employed electricians, plumbers and builders. However, there were unintended beneficiaries – and many of these were from the creative industries.

Jazzie used the scheme to build his sound system and take it to increasingly large venues around London. With his work in clubs and on radio, his music collective Soul II Soul became a big force in the creation of the British club scene. Their distinctive sound made them chart-topping superstars. For some people, their UK number 1 hit 'Back to Life' is *the* sound of the 1980s. Jazzie B also created a fashion line – Funki Dred – which captured and marketed a black British street style. His brand mantra was: 'A happy face, a thumping bass, for a loving race.' He was upbeat, enterprising and very successful.

The music was great and went head-to-head with the Americans and Jamaicans. I remember going to a club in New York where the highlights were all tracks by Soul II Soul. The Yanks hadn't a clue that this was British music. Suddenly we were not only proud to be black and British, but we were part of a mainstream culture that made money. Like Mary Seacole and Levi Roots, Jazzie B was a walking, living example of his own brand – in his case, a Funki Dred preaching Thatcher's new culture of enterprise.

Here was a wonderful synergy of the new cultural hybridity of Britain with good old Conservative capitalism. This was not a strange brew for Jazzie: he saw how the multicultural energy of Britain was linked to enterprise culture. In many ways,

Jazzie was ahead of his time. If you think of the way business is done on the internet, it combines globalisation with disruptive new trading models. Jazzie took multiculturalism and British hybridity and packaged them into a brand that could be sold internationally. Black Britain became a prototype for Cool Britannia. He says:

> And I guess from them early days we had the ambition and drive to know what we wanted to achieve, and the next stage was really about Soul II Soul being like an international sound system where our music will be played in as many places as possible.
>
> It probably was difficult to bring British music to people who listened to Jamaican music, but for me there was a time where everybody was saturated by the whole popular music … I think the conscious decision with Soul II Soul, taking it into the mainstream is just simply like this: we wanted to play to more but we couldn't … So as well as making our own dubs and specials, we just wanted to get our sound to a larger audience.[14]

It was this energy, this determination to move from the 'community centre' to centre stage, that made Soul II Soul so successful. Of the music itself, he says:

> I think Soul II Soul is far more like a British sound than a London sound because there's been people all over the UK globe that have been involved in Soul II Soul, so I think it'd be very one-dimensional to suggest that Soul II Soul is just a London thing. We are more of a British thing. I mean, now black Britain has all types of things to be proud of. I think

I'm a bit of both really. I'm black and I'm definitely British and that's what I am.[15]

What I love about Jazzie B is that there's no identity anxiety. He is not only British, but his sound has been part of Britain's development. He's not on a decolonisation war, trying to tear down the old guard who represent all that's oppressive. He's doing something new. There is confidence in the British space, with all its varied influences.

FREEDOM, AGENCY, BRITAIN

There's often a freedom among black musicians in Britain. They tend to be confident in their own, uniquely British, skins. British musicians have always drawn on all the global influences that surround them, and this effect has been catalysed in recent years through the porous pages of the internet. Soul II Soul were the first to put a distinct black British sound on the map, but the effect has only accelerated since then. Today, British artists fuse sounds from the whole world into a distinctive, confident and outward-looking new style.

In the 1980s, Jazzie B took me to the promised land; he helped a generation to understand how to be free. His exhortation to 'elevate your mind, free your soul' is needed today more than ever. As an American race lobby seeks to trap us in identitarian misery, Jazzie exhorts us to an act of self-actualisation: as Marley says, none but 'ourselves' can free our minds. To be free in this sense means to draw on the great power of agency – and Mary Seacole, Jazzie B, and Levi Roots are all perfect exemplars of doing just that. They use their agency to create a sense of freedom. They literally 'do what they want'. It's an enormously attractive, and therefore often lucrative, way to be in the world. One version of black success, then, is a yoking of the Caribbean attitude and culture to what we might describe as the British 'shopkeepers of the world' mentality.

It's frustrating that *this* story hasn't been told in schools. They wrongly stuck the label of Mary Seacole on nursing schools and made her arm-wrestle Florence Nightingale, mainly because we overlook and denigrate black people who make money and work within the capitalist system. We think our children need a saintly, self-sacrificing Mary Seacole so they can stand proud in racist Britain. They don't. Seacole needs to be redrawn not as an antidote to Florence Nightingale, nor as a flawed medical practitioner, but as the serious international businesswoman that she was: a moneymaker and barrier-breaker.

In Bennett's poem 'Colonisation in Reverse', we also see a Seacole-like Caribbean spirit. In terms of the post-war generation, she is talking about a developing market: the new buyers and sellers who would soon be homeowners, who would soon develop their own music industry, grow their own informal banking system, build their own churches and support their home economies through remittances. The motive and the drive behind this had nothing to do with a patriotic eagerness to build back the British economy. It was about building their own wealth. Ironically, what the Windrush Generation found when they arrived in Britain was the capacity to build and nurture themselves as a community.

It is to them that we look next when thinking about black success. Throughout my life, my parents' generation has been a great source of inspiration to me. The Windrush Generation, like the heroes in a Greek epic, have lived stories of defiance, opportunism, resilience and courage. And in the next chapter we're going to look more deeply at them and at those characteristics, to ask what they might mean for black success. Principally, we'll look at an area of black success in Britain that is too often overlooked: property.

7

THE HOUSING LARK
HOW A PEOPLE BUILT THEIR FUTURE

I want a capital-earning democracy. Every man and woman a capitalist. Housing is the start. If you're a man or woman of property, you've got something. So, every man a capitalist, and every man a man of property.

—Margaret Thatcher

W HEN I interviewed several black Caribbean pioneers who migrated to the UK between the 1940s and the 1960s, one thing was clear: none of them came to Britain as a result of a calling from the mother country. These were not 'colonials' with a passion to keep the home fires burning. Primarily, they were young people on an adventure, seeking opportunities and a better standard of living.

The other thing they had in common was that by 1981 all had 'regulated' their citizenship status, converting their Dependent Territories passports into full British ones. I point this out because they, like my parents, represent the majority who were not victims of the Windrush scandal. I remember the day my mother posted off her old passport, grumbling about the fee she had to pay, and how a few weeks later my parents received their new passports and citizenship. There was a deadline and I remember the sense of urgency within the community.

The scandal began in 2018 and mainly impacted those from the Caribbean. It came about in the context of the British government getting tough on illegal migration and was never intended to hit the longstanding Caribbean group. Nevertheless, the Home Office failed to see the implications, which had an impact on all those who, for whatever reason, did not have the right documentation. They were suddenly denied work and medical support, and a large number were threatened with deportation. Later a compensation scheme was set up so that those who lost out could get payments and full citizenship. The majority were insulated from the Windrush scandal because they regularised their status when told to.

Daphne Steel was born in Guyana but came to the UK to make a career. When I interviewed her, I immediately got the sense of a proud woman. Her father was a pharmacist and this gave her a taste for the medical professions. In even her earliest memories, she recalls wanting to be a nurse. Her sister is the well-known actress Carmen Monroe, who also came to Britain, where she starred in the hit comedy *Desmond's*.

When she came to this country Daphne was not escaping poverty (Guyana was doing well economically); she just wanted to advance her career. She recalls:

> It took 14 days by boat, and we landed at Plymouth. We were met by a British Council official. The first thing that struck me was that a white man took my luggage and began pushing it. No white people worked in Guyana. They all had managerial

posts and would never get their hands dirty. I couldn't get used to the terraced housing. And the women on their knees cleaning the front steps. In Guyana we had people to clean for us.

She did her training in London. Like many black nurses, she faced racism from white colleagues and patients. This discrimination and ignorance often came in the most unexpected ways: 'One sister asked a black colleague to take a plate out of the oven and couldn't understand why she needed an oven glove. She really believed she would be able to stand the heat.'

As far as the patients were concerned, Daphne went on a charm offensive to disarm their racism. This worked well for her, and she always refused to take the bait, no matter what the provocation. However, she did admit that sometimes what they needed was a good 'cussing':

I did admire the Jamaican nurses for this, they didn't stand for any nonsense. We used to have Jamaican nurses fighting our battles. If a nurse felt that somebody was bullying her – a Jamaican nurse would say, 'Point me in that person's direction. Who is it, let me go and tell her about her ******.'

Encouraged by a friendly Irish matron, Daphne applied for and got a job as a matron herself, at St Winifred's Hospital in Ilkley, West Yorkshire. In 1964 she became Britain's first black matron. 'I earned that job – it was not a token appointment,' she says.

For others, the complex experience of migration sparked and spurred their creativity. The leading Jamaican poet James Berry captures the ambiguity of the migrant experience in much of his work. An early migrant to Britain, he writes in his poem 'Thoughts of My Father' about the limitations and passivity of life in the

Caribbean – 'an earth loving rock'. Like my parents, he was desperate for movement and change. The poem ends with the words

> I must assemble material
> of my own
> for a new history.[1]

This, I believe, sums up the drive in the minds of my parents'
generation: a need to make your own world and create your
own history. There was a sense that Europeans had been busy
changing history in the colonies, but that poor black people
were just marking time. In the poem Berry sees himself as
arresting time, making time work for him. It reminds me once
again of that phrase Jamaican DJs cry out: 'We run tings, tings
nuh run we'. For Berry, running tings meant leaving home and
making history in another land.

Berry came to England in 1948 on the *Orbita*, the ship
that followed the *Windrush*. In his writings he recalls how his
father's passivity fuelled his own desire to depart. His father, he
said, 'was so stuck in the "plantation mentality" that education
for him would have been a waste of time'. Berry began to 'dread'
becoming like him: 'He became a symbol of why I had to leave
Jamaica, he represented the life that I hated. I loved stories
but no one was going to buy me a book. He was symbolic of a
culture of acceptance.'

Berry wanted more than acceptance. He wanted knowledge.
He wanted a history and a future. He explains: 'We had no
sense of history. I played on the ruins of the old slave mill and
didn't know what it was. There was such a strong shame of
slavery, there was no process of handing anything down. The
world of my father was his machete, his donkey and his land.

I had no idea about my ancestors and what happened to them. In school we had no black heroes.'

Berry was desperate to find a new space in which he could hone his writing craft and come to understand his own history. He does not mince his words about the depressing nature of life in post-war Jamaica:

> I could see that in my village if there was a ship big enough, everyone would want to get away. There was something about the spirit of the place that had so undermined the people's psychology that they felt they could only make it elsewhere. What I wanted was opportunity, in my village there was no opportunity. People were never going to make it.

So Berry came to London and became a poet. His early poems – collected in his first book *Fractured Circle* (1979) – chart the life of West Indian immigrants in the London of the 1950s. Life in London is in some ways bleak: the doors slammed in black faces by affronted white landladies, the hustle for work and warmth, the ongoing racism. But what his poems also capture, uniquely, is the spirit of adventure and elation that the 'country boy' making life in the big city retained, despite all the setbacks. So the poem 'Migrant in London' declares:

> I stan' in the roar, man,
> in a dream of wheels
> a-vibrate shadows.
> I feel how wheels hurry in wheels
>
> I whisper, man you mek it.
> You arrive.

> Then sudden like, quite loud I say,
> 'Then whey you goin' sleep tonight?'[2]

I love this poem. It speaks to the complex experience of the first pioneer adventurers to Britain. It is, in some sense, the ultimate journey narrative – where a physical journey runs parallel to a journey of self-discovery. Berry's migrant in London is finding himself and finding his capacity to build a community. Of course, it was a very tough environment, where racism was still persistent. He says:

> I was born in colonial Jamaica. From about ten years old – through my schoolbooks, through the white family who towered over us and my own village people – I began to pick up attitudes and beliefs that frightened me. I began to see that I inherited a slave history that made my parents, my village and myself feel unquestionably inferior. So perhaps my writing is my struggle, to find, to claim and to celebrate my humanity.

James managed to find a good job but was eventually able to write full-time. His books have sold worldwide and, in 1990, he was awarded the OBE for his contribution to poetry. Not bad for a Jamaican peasant boy who played on the slave mills and came to Britain to find and tell his story. That story is a truly inspiring one. Berry found liberation from the confinement of colonial Jamaica when he came to Britain. He linked up with other writers and became part of a Caribbean writer's movement in the 1960s. For all its persistent racism, Britain was nevertheless a place of creativity, possibility and success.

Finally, there's Bishop Joe Aldred. He came to Britain from Jamaica in the 1960s, aged 15, to meet up with his parents who had gone ahead. What he found in Britain was the usual racism – both inside and outside the church. A strongly religious man, Joe was soon to be a bishop within his own denomination, a strand of black Pentecostalism called the Church of God.

There is an oversimple narrative about black people and the church in the UK. It goes like this: black people arrived in Britain, went along to their local white church and were given the cold shoulder by a hostile congregation. This led them to go away and set up their own churches. Joe loves exploding this myth. What really happened, he says, is that the Caribbean church, in all its many variations, was already well established at home and people simply replanted their old church in a new country. They wanted business as usual and that meant the continuation of their own denomination. These churches each had their own doctrine and culture, which would have been different not only from mainstream white churches but also from the other black churches on offer.

What frustrates Joe, who will always remind you that he is still living in Babylon, is how these myths always position black people as mega-victims. The black church in Britain is not a story of victimhood: it is a story of astonishing success. In fact, black churches quickly became so powerful that in many cases they bought the buildings of white churches, which today struggle to be viable. He speaks passionately about the continuation of racialised discrimination. However, he refuses to allow this kind of racism to define him. He had to break down historic barriers, and he did.

Joe speaks wonderfully of his Pentecostal background, in a radical and empowering way. For him, Pentecost is all about receiving the Spirit, the power of being anointed. He doesn't deny the reality of racism, but his agency means it doesn't define or defeat him:

> Finding myself in this Babylon, I must look to myself, not to white people. It's not the reality of the situation, it's about how to respond. You cannot take away my humanity. Make something of the space that you are within. You get a grip; you can do something about your situation. Even the *Windrush* ... it has become moneymaking ... your best advocate is you. There is an energy ... reggae music is not about others, it's about liberating yourself. The emphasis [is] on agency and self-help. The people who do the advocacy don't really cede benefit to the people, they only end up improving themselves.

When I interviewed him in Leeds, Joe felt that some politicians were not very helpful when it comes to the *Windrush* legacy. He said:

> They don't want to change ... the Left is about deconstruction. We need to construct, have our own agency and community. All of our great minds are spent studying the faults of white people. Build your own I say ... we are agreeing with the white racists. They invited us and now they are kicking us ... in fact they didn't want the ship to dock back in 1948. The narrative is a far cry from success ... it simply says unless white people stop being racist, there is nothing we can do.

Three stories. Three successes. The usual traits that we associate with immigrant success stories are abundant here: grit, guile, creativity, resourcefulness. But there is something slightly out of view and unexpected that underpins these stories, and the successes of the Windrush Generation more generally.

Property.

Arguably, the space in which Caribbean people in Britain have been most successful is not their careers, however impressive these may have been. Healthcare, creative writing and an enormously powerful church have all offered opportunities, garlands and a stake in British life. But the bedrock of black success, particularly in the pioneer generation, has been in the quintessentially British pursuit of property and home ownership. It was a success won against all the odds.

MAKE A HOUSE A HOME

When Caribbean settlers arrived in the UK, they were excluded from housing because of racism and prejudice. Landlords were allowed to discriminate openly against West Indians. In 1965 the Milner Committee[3] reported that 27% of landlords directly barred black applicants and only 6% of housing owners indicated that black people were welcome. When it came to council housing, Caribbean settlers were absent because of racist resident restrictions. It wasn't until the implementation of the 1968 Race Relations Act that the practice of discrimination was made illegal.

The fact of racial discrimination in housing is well known. What is less well known is how many of the Windrush Generation responded to that rejection. Take the example of Alford Gardner. Alford, a Jamaican, joined the RAF during the Second World War and had 'a cracking time in Britain, especially with the local women'. When he was demobbed, he returned to Jamaica, but found 'not enough jobs, bad pay, tough conditions'. So he left for England, in June 1948, aboard the SS *Empire Windrush*.

Alford speaks positively of life on board the *Windrush*, which he found relaxing. He had to pay £28, which took care of food and board. There were only a few women, some of whom had romances with the English sailors. Most of his shipmates were like him: young men in their twenties who were looking forward to this new adventure. According to Alford, most of the people who had boarded the *Windrush* had jobs and friends waiting for them in England. But there was one difficulty: accommodation. Housing was difficult to come by as landladies fretted about what their neighbours might say if they took in 'coloured' lodgers. He was repeatedly refused lodgings. Alford's solution? He and four friends decided to club together and buy their own house, which they would share. For many West Indians, it turned out that it was easier to buy than rent. What they couldn't know was that the large, rundown places they bought cheaply would turn into goldmines as prosperity turned the inner cities into desirable places to live. Put simply: in Brixton during the early 1960s, a small house would cost maybe £1,000. By the mid-1990s, the same property would be worth around £100,000.

Alford and his friends are like the real-life counterparts of the enterprising West Indians in *The Housing Lark*, a humorous novel by Trinidadian writer Sam Selvon.[4] In *The Housing Lark*, the hero, Battersby, sits in his cramped basement room in Brixton dreaming of money, women, a T-bone steak – and a place to call his own. So he and a group of friends decide to save up and buy a house together. Despite racism, backbiting and the temptation to spend the cash, they eventually get their house. Selvon was not trying to romanticise the experience of the early migrants: his point was that, once in England, immigrants had agency and could respond positively to their circumstances. His novel speaks not only of the immigrants' ambition but also of their determination not to lose their 'character' or 'humanity', much of this being rooted in their Caribbean sense of community.

A person who could have stepped straight from the pages of *The Housing Lark* is Joe Whitter. He came from Jamaica in 1954 and became Britain's first black property entrepreneur. He bought his first house in Forest Hill, South London, an area I know well. Joe has done extraordinarily well in Britain. Many will dismiss his success as a one-off or the exception to the rule. But what is clear from his story, and what makes it representative of so many others, is the way in which housing can be used as a means of social mobility in Britain. For poor people, property ownership removes most of the usual barriers to gaining wealth and acquiring social capital. It can fast-track you into security, and even income, at the same time that it does away with the vagaries and difficulties that come from renting a home. In an interview for writer Mike Phillips, Joe says:

Well, I went to England in the fifties –1954 – and of course, I was looking for a better life. I was a young man, and I wanted to see what the outside world was like, and it was a good thing that I did go to England. I do all sorts of jobs. I can remember my first job in England was to work in the park. I then go on to dig the street up, you know, and from there, the sheepskin factory, the bakery. I became a haulage contractor; I own a number of trucks. And you name it, I've done it, in England, and I enjoy it.

Well, I could remember, I saw a lot of West Indian folks buying properties and tried to find out more … They were buying these houses, renting them out to their fellow West Indians, and were making a package. Within about three months, I bought four properties. And then within forty-five years, I owned the most property of any black man in the country. Something like 400 houses, all over England.

Well, the heart of doing this, and a lot of people didn't sort of realise, I go along, and I will buy, say five homes, for £5,000. I'll go to the bank, and I will get the £5,000 – a hundred per cent mortgage. I would convert those houses – if they're four storeys, I'll probably put them into four flats. And then I would sell one flat for, you know, what I paid for five houses. And I still retained the freehold of the property. And then I went to buy the next ten houses, I'd then go back and use that property as, of course, the collateral to buy. So, to me, it was really a game. Understand the tricks, how you do it, the timing, and believe you me, it was great.[5]

Joe Whitter said that he always felt that England was his home. He managed to buy himself, at the age of 20, a 20-bedroom mansion in Bromley. He also loved his grand Rolls-Royce. He returned to Jamaica in 1980 and went into business there, but still owns many properties in Britain, where his five children remain.

In her oral history *When I Came to England*, Nia Reynolds spoke to Tom Evans, who recalled how difficult it was to find housing – the indignity of knocking on a door only to be turned away by a racist landlord once he saw your skin colour. Tom arrived in England from Jamaica in 1963:

It was very difficult in those days trying to find somewhere to live. I was looking to get a place with at least three rooms and in most of the paper shops you would see them advertising flats for rent and when you go and knock, they would say, 'It's gone,' although it wasn't.[6]

His fortunes were to change after a conversation with his white landlord:

He said, 'Why not buy it?' I said that I didn't have money to buy it. He said, 'The same money you pay me for rent can buy it.' Then he said he would give me a mortgage ... At that time houses didn't value [weren't worth] anything because the first house that I bought had six bedrooms and two bathrooms, kitchen and sitting room. And I paid £4,500 for it. Now you would pay £3.5 million.[7]

The moral of his tale is *not* to justify the discrimination. The racism should not have been allowed to happen. But the power of Tom Evans's story, and all the others like it, is in how, through luck and managing risk, he managed to turn housing rejection into housing prosperity. As Bob Marley sang, 'When one door is closed, many more is open.'

RIGHTS TO BUY

It may seem paradoxical, but black success has often arisen when (as Marcus Garvey would say) 'our backs are against the wall'. The opportunity to turn a disadvantage into an advantage is not always available, of course, and sometimes the law needs to be changed. However, black success, like any successful strategy, depends on the ability to choose between a variety of options. My parents' generation were smart enough to turn their housing crisis to their economic advantage. The disadvantage of being excluded from housing on the basis of colour prejudice was seared deeply into their memory. Yet they achieved housing success through a combination of partner schemes (a community-based saving system) and renting out part of their home.

I remember, as a young man during the early 1990s, the day my mother ran into the living room with a letter in her hand screaming as if she had won the lottery. It was a letter from the Greater London Council saying that my parents had paid off their mortgage and were now title holders. I felt proud of them; they had worked so hard and now they were sitting on valuable real estate. Champagne corks must have popped across many Caribbean families at around this time, as they finally shed their mortgage debts and found themselves with a home of their own. My parents' journey ended well.

The housing story for those early Caribbean settlers is, then, a complex one. But from the perspective of today it looks like a relative success. I knew from my own experience, and those of my peers, that our parents owned their homes at the same, if not greater, level than their white counterparts. Historians point to racism in the private rental market as the reason why black people bought their own homes. But one can also point at poor access to social housing: here, Caribbean newcomers were not even considered. In 1984 local authorities were forced by the Commission for Racial Equality (CRE) to drop their 'sons and daughters' rule, a policy whereby children could inherit tenancies from their dead parents even if they now lived elsewhere. The policy was judged to be discriminatory against ethnic minority groups and often led in practice to ethnic segregation. Most social housing went to white families, while black people had to deal with the vagaries of an unregulated private sector. Growing up in Penge, I saw that most of the council estates were white and that most of my black friends lived in owner-occupier housing.

Looking at the 1962 Census microdata (a sample of c. 5%) is the best way of unpacking this statistically. The Windrush group is here defined loosely as immigrants from the Caribbean living in Britain. In 1961, 48.6% of Jamaicans lived in homes that were owner-occupied, compared to 40.7% of all those born in England, 42.6% of those born in Australia and 53% of those from India.[8]

If you then look at the data from 1994, it appears that the Caribbean population are falling behind relative to 1961 – a time when racial hostility was much greater. It seems the real issue here is the fragmentation of the Caribbean family, with many of my own generation living in single-occupant council housing rather than in owner-occupation.[9] The good news from the 1994 data is that many Caribbean people took advantage of the Thatcher-inspired 'right to buy': 23% of Caribbean homeowners were formerly in council homes, compared to 14% of whites and 4% of Indians.

The Windrush Generation still show relatively good numbers on home ownership, given that many have died or decided to sell up and go back to the Caribbean. Lazy and politically driven researchers lump the Caribbean data on housing in with the data of newer African migrants to show evidence of racism. The reality is that new populations arriving in the expensive city of London, some of them refugees, do not have the means to buy their own homes and are forced to rent. The data shows Caribbeans are more likely to be owner-occupiers compared to African groups, particularly when you control for age – or, to put it another way, when you consider how long people have been here. A research paper by the Race Equality Foundation shows that a high level of owner-occupation continues among the Caribbean group, compared to other ethnicities. In 2011 more than 90% of African Caribbean people aged 50 to 60 owned their homes. This compared to 70% of black African and 75% of white 'other ethnic' groups.[10]

HOW 'BRITISH WEST INDIANS' COLONISED AMERICAN REAL ESTATE

The story of the British colonial period is not just one of black suffering and white privilege. Caribbean people fought back, and their resistance was often tactical and smart. One of the more surprising ways in which they did this was the acquisition of property and land in America, enabling them to build generational wealth. In America today Caribbean people occupy a prominent place in the black middle class. In a brilliant paper for the *George Washington Law Review*, Eleanor Marie Brown poses a fascinating question:

> Why are the black brownstone owners in Harlem and Brooklyn disproportionately West Indian? The landlords West Indian-American? The tenants African-American? These are tough questions. For students of housing discrimination, West Indian Americans have long presented a quandary. If it is reasonable to assume that racial exclusions are being consistently

applied to persons who are dark-skinned, one would expect to find that housing discrimination has had similar effects on West Indian-Americans and African-Americans. Yet this is not the case: West Indian-Americans generally own and rent higher quality housing than African-Americans.[11]

To unravel these questions we must go back to the 1920s. Sociological studies have found that there was a tendency at this time for West Indians (I use the term as a historic reference, aware that it is now dated) to confidently set up home in better quality districts than African-Americans. In fact, they often settled in former white middle-class areas, where lots of property was available. Eventually, many moved up and bought into predominantly white neighbourhoods. In New York, West Indians would often buy whole blocks of housing and hold these in trust for others until they arrived.

With this accumulation of property, West Indians effectively became the gatekeepers of black housing. In doing so, they tore up the segregation playbook: they knew that money talks and buys houses, and to this extent they were doing integration well before Martin Luther King. The question now becomes: what was so special about West Indians, that they could do this? For me, one answer is that they saw themselves as 'British West Indians'. They were able to play insider-outsider to the white power base that monopolised the housing stock. Yes, they were black – but they were not African-American. This gave them the confidence to approach white property owners and strike up amazing deals, which in time brought them a significant degree of control over the New York property market.

There were several important ways in which the West Indians differed from African-Americans. For one, they were more confident, as they had not experienced racism in quite the same way, coming from black-majority countries. This helped them to break up the exclusive white monopoly on home ownership and create their own monopoly among West Indians. It is clear that West Indian people in America never really saw themselves as 'black' (or in those days 'Negro'). They were 'West Indian', with a mindset and confidence that enabled them to bypass American segregation laws. This has continued right up until today, when Jamaicans form part of a strong middle class and have become a great success story within America.

Perhaps most importantly, the West Indians were able to play the market because they knew how to accumulate cash. Ironically, they learnt this strategy from their dealings with white plantation owners after slavery, when the owners sold off their estates to black people who pooled their money and made cash offers for land.

Officially, the ex-slaves had been given one choice on emancipation: work to remain on the land. Under this system, the planter would 'lease' the land to the newly freed slave in return for a share of the crops (or some other in-kind payment). There was also a nasty system called 'apprenticeship', in which ex-slaves had to work on the land for a few more years, in a kind of transition period, before they gained full freedom. But these systems never really worked, and in truth many simply walked off the estates and 'captured' land elsewhere – while others struck deals with the planters in which groups of former slaves became landowners themselves. Decades later, their descendants used these assets to raise money and do similar transactions in New York, this time for urban real estate. West Indians were well placed to persuade white property owners to break away from their white-only property club. Rules and laws around segregation soon melted away as these new black people were able to do cash deals.

Even at its height, the slave system in the Caribbean was different from that in America. Under the so-called 'provision ground' system, the enslaved were given plots of land to grow their own provisions, which encouraged land ownership and agency.

At this stage I want to put out a warning. Some are so soaked in victimhood that they will take the last paragraph as meaning that I am justifying slavery or colonialism. What I have actually said is that Jamaicans were able to use their past, however brutalised and tortured, to create advantages once they migrated to America. This obviously doesn't justify the brutality of slavery; but it does challenge the usual narrative that our colonial past destroyed our souls and agency. Many have recorded slavery's negative legacy, in realities like 'colourism' or the fact that planters were given compensation for their so-called loss after emancipation. What hasn't been shared is that early Caribbean land ownership by ex-slaves helped restore them to confidence, dignity and wealth. When they arrived in America, West Indians never saw themselves as second-class citizens of their new country. Rather, they identified as British West Indians and many refused to give up their British passports.

What is fascinating about this 'West Indian-American' story is that it breaks the usual narrative of encounters between blacks and whites. Yes, there is white dominance – but in America it soon turns to black dominance within a capitalist framework. One particular black group captures the market, using all the tools that ethnic whites would have used in their determination to be property tycoons. The Italians and Jews came to this market with their own background strengths; the

West Indians came as British. What is remarkable is that this happened in the 1920s.

It seems to me that this history would have encouraged later Caribbean migrants to Britain to see the purchase of housing as a means not just of acquiring shelter but also of wealth creation. What seems to have changed for my generation was the introduction of priority council housing, which incentivised single motherhood and spelled the end for reliable fatherhood. This, combined with mass unemployment, knocked the enterprise stuffing out of a generation. We never really recovered. We never were able to build the intergenerational wealth that became a feature of our Caribbean cousins in America. On a personal note, I have followed the example of my role models across the pond and bought several properties in America using credit and confidence.

In Britain I have personally benefited from the enterprise and luck of a generation that invested in housing stock – even if this was partly out of forced circumstance. This aspect of the Caribbean migrant experience is indeed a good news story, one that shows a plucky group of prospectors making their own fortunes.

Journeys to new lands, ships, exodus, quests are at the heart of the Caribbean experience. It is what makes us part of the modern project. This restlessness is, of course, often driven by terrible economic and social conditions, but it has nonetheless proved an incredible creative, innovative force. This energy travelled to Britain and replanted itself here, flowering in the music, churches, writing, humour and general culture of post-1950s Britain. It is also this can-do spirit that leads to survival strategies in the moment that pay off decades down the line.

THE RETURN JOURNEY

Most of those who came to Britain in the 1950s thought they would make some quick money and return home within three years. That's why it's wrong to see them as somehow conned by the British. They never expected the racism and exclusion – but neither was their voyage to Britain a noble sacrifice, a duty of service to King and Country. They just wanted to make a better life for themselves. None would have dreamed that their modest houses, bought because there were no better options, would make them millionaires. By the 1980s, many were channelling money back home, to support relatives and perhaps help them buy housing on the other side of the Atlantic.

Home ownership in the UK also translated into the phenomenon of wealthy returnees to the Caribbean. Not only were they able to cash in on their housing investment in the UK and buy fantastic properties in the Caribbean, but many also had great incomes from their London Transport, British Rail or other public sector pensions. During the 1990s, those pensions went a long way internationally, given the strength of the pound.

What does the journey's end look like for those early settlers? The answer is as complex, varied and ambiguous as their experiences as migrants to the UK. Success takes many forms, and the return to Jamaica reflects the full range of these experiences. Some return to the area they left, even to the house they were born in. Many buy land and build their dream houses, often white mansions with multiple bedrooms, bathrooms and landscaped gardens. Some opt for gated communities complete with high security. The equity from even a modest

UK home – such as an ex-council flat – can be converted into something much more upscale in the Caribbean. Many fold back into their old lifestyles, catching up with relatives and friends from childhood. Others build connections with other returnees, becoming expats in the country they were born in. Many talk of 'giving back'; for example, I have met teachers who made their careers in Britain now working to improve education in the Caribbean.

Jamaica – along with other Caribbean islands – was quick to see the financial potential in this older, wealthier demographic. From the late 1970s, the UK version of the *Jamaica Gleaner* newspaper was full of advertising from property developers enticing Jamaicans abroad to invest in schemes like Willowdene in Spanish Town. One of them had a housing scheme in St Thomas, where the roads were called Tottenham Hale and Finsbury Park. A big housing development on the north coast was called Richmond. I was reminded of some of the 'mother-country' propaganda used by London Transport in the 1960s to encourage young people from the Caribbean to come to Britain. One set of adverts sold the idea of idyllic retirement to Jamaica, another held out the promise of money and opportunity in good old London.

In a seminal piece of research on British/Caribbean returnees, Heather Ayn Horst focussed on the town of Mandeville in central Jamaica.[12] This is known for its rolling hills and (for Jamaica) very cool climate. I used to teach English to high school pupils in a nearby town called Spaldings. According to Horst, Mandeville is 'unofficially noted as the "Returning Resident Capital of Jamaica"' and 'represents a nodal point for studying returnees' engagements with the people and places of a changed Jamaica'.

Migration, in whatever direction, is never without its difficulties. Horst's interview subjects talk frequently, and often at length, of the challenge of reintegration, of building issues, and of missing grandchildren, Tetley's tea and Heinz baked beans. They worry about the lack of an NHS, the threat of violence made even more alarming by the lurid media coverage of crime, and the very different, often hard-to-navigate infrastructure of Jamaica's systems and institutions.

According to Horst, the relationship with the local communities could become problematic: the returnees can be perceived as rich and arrogant 'foreigners' who are not as generous as Americans, and who walk too fast. In response, many returnees bought into stereotypes around Jamaicans, branding them as 'lazy', untrustworthy and unreliable. Indeed, she notes how stereotypes on both sides tend to dominate their interactions:

> Most 'locals', who describe returnees as 'the English', note returnees' airs of superiority, particularly the superiority concerning how bureaucracy and services are 'better' in England. Some of the shopkeepers admitted being very frustrated with the returnee tendency to pinch every penny, not trust anyone, and some helpers complain that returnees overwork them. Goulbourne (1999) discusses the tendency to view returnees as 'mad hatters' running around town in their funny dress and funny accents and a number of people asked me to 'find out why returnees are so mad' or 'miserable'.[13]

It is somewhat ironic that these people were subject to racist stereotypes when they first came to England – and now they are back in Jamaica, they are resented for being arrogant foreigners. Some ignore it, some slow down and learn new approaches, while others have developed their own social groups and residential associations.

In a gated community in the parish of St Ann's, returnees make up over half the occupants. They find comfort in their common experience, even setting up the 'M1 Club' as a reminder of the iconic motorway that links the south and the north of Britain. As in many of these communities, the residents spend a large proportion of their time away in the UK or America. The properties are bought for a variety of purposes – some for reasons of sentimentality (just to have a piece of the rock), some for that eventual retirement, others as a retreat from the ravages of the British or American winter. For them Britain is 'home', a country in which they feel fully integrated.

These people came to Britain and helped to change it, but Britain also changed them. The returnees, in all their variety, deserve a medal. They now have global, emotional and financial obligations across the diaspora. They form a powerful group whose assets have helped the foreign currency of many Caribbean islands. They have made huge profits for Caribbean banks, while on the UK home front they are still in great demand for grandparenting duties and as a kind of reserve Bank of Mum and Dad. This is a group that has seen their own desire for retirement become another global adventure.

It would be safe to say that most of these settlers recognise a different and better Britain today from the one they arrived in. The pull for them to return was an ancestral one, rather than a hatred for racist Britain. In Jamaica, children often hear adults say, 'Mih navel string bury right 'ere.' This refers to a practice in which, after birth, the navel string is buried in the yard, to connect the child to their home. A return is always sentimental. Just as leaving, for James Berry, expressed a kind of yearning, these returns represent an equal and opposite yearning. For many, then, there is a kind of conflict within their success. Many will tell you that despite the racism they have had a positive journey in Britain. They are now left with a double yearning – for their grandchildren in Britain and their homeland in the Caribbean.

THE HOUSING LARK

Whichever way you slice it, the so-called 'Housing Lark' sheltered (if you'll excuse the pun) a generation from the madness and brutality of white racism. Indirectly, it became the means for many to return to the Caribbean and begin yet another adventure, this time in the land of their birth. Yet we often overlook housing and the intergenerational wealth, not to mention security, that came with it, when we tell the stories of black people in Britain, particularly the indomitable Windrush Generation. Why is this? I think it's for all the reasons that British people are generally cagey about class – and not least because this sort of success requires a certain amount of good fortune to be thrown in among the guile, determination and grit.

As I wrote earlier, I believe that there are three traits that lead to black success. The first of these is *Flipping a narrative of negativity into one of positivity*. I fear that we have a tendency to be negative when telling the story of the black British experience, and as a result we can feel like perpetual victims. But the arrival of the Windrush Generation should not simply be seen as a negative one of racist landlords, abuse and humiliation. It is also the story of buccaneering adventurers who went out into the world and succeeded against the odds. Today, the last laugh is with those who were forced into property ownership because the door was slammed in their faces by racists.

Even when we tell a positive tale – when we look at successes like Daphne Steel, James Berry and Joe Aldred – we don't always tell the whole story. The way in which we think about the Windrush Generation is inflected with a kind of nostalgia and overfamiliarity. The story that we are familiar with focusses on success outside the home – for Daphne, James and Joe, in the worlds of nursing, poetry and the church. But we are perhaps not as familiar with the private success that their generation had as prudent investors, sharp negotiators and smart opportunists. That's a shame, because when we do look at this very real black success, we see suddenly that it is right there in the centre of mainstream British life. There is an inspirational story on practically every street of our great cities.

That story is predicated on flipping a negative experience – exclusion, discrimination, racism – into a positive one. Security. Wealth. Success.

As mentioned, this story then goes full circle, with many using the gains from property wealth in Britain to retire to the Caribbean. While that's not exactly my story, I have, in recent years, channelled my inner Odysseus and become the hero of my own return journey.

In the final chapter of this book, we move to Jamaica, and to my farm, to look holistically at black success, reaping what you sow and being the author of your own story.

Our return is not just the quasi-spiritual one that I have engaged in, returning to the land my father left. We'll also return to the document that kicked this book off: the Report of the Commission on Race and Ethnic Disparities.

8

ODYSSEUS AND THE FIVE TALENTS
REAPING WHAT YOU SOW

I N 2020 the former West Indies cricketing great, now pundit, Michael Holding chose the break in a game on Sky television to unleash his feelings on race and racism. His position as a successful cricketer and a television commentator would appear to make him immune to everyday racism. But he wanted to tell us otherwise.

His 'coming out' was the usual story of limitation and defeat. He cited the example of how the black scientist George Latymer had been edited out of the history books, which give all the glory for the invention of the light bulb to Thomas Edison. We are to assume that the reason white people feel superior to black people is that they have been programmed to see the latter as inferior.

But Holding could have told a very different story. He could have referred to the great victory in which he had played a defining part; a victory that coincided with the new popularity of reggae music and the Caribbean emerging with a real sense of independence from the madness of the colonial era. In

1976 the West Indies team came to England and spent nearly a whole year resoundingly defeating the home side in both Test matches and one-day contests. It was a heady time, one of optimism, pride and the sweet smell of cricketing victory. Holding could have celebrated the success of the West Indian cricket side that he played in. He could have added that this wasn't fuelled by slogans of black pride, but that it had come from new, world-beating levels of professionalism and skill.

I didn't want Michael Holding to deny the reality of racism; but I would have liked him to remind us that he and his team were winners. We needed to hear how his West Indies side had conquered the world and inspired a generation.

Elsewhere, Holding is happy to give us some clues about how all this was achieved. Asked whether his great West Indies side was held back by racism in 1976, he replies:

> During my entire career as a cricketer playing for the West Indies, no one on the cricket field passed a racist remark towards me. People will say because you bowled fast, they were afraid. But I don't think that was the case. We in that team never said anything to anyone, we never abused anyone on the cricket field. Perhaps that is the reason why people didn't really say anything to us. Because all that we did was go about our business and play as well as we possibly could.[1]

They were not limited by racism because the game was a fair one and talent prevailed. The team triumphed without everyone needing to read the *Autobiography of Malcolm X* before they came out to bat.

Like so many in 2020, Michael was caught up in the George Floyd emotion. Yes, we did need a black history lesson, but it was not one about who invented light bulbs. For him, the moment unearthed the real racism that existed, and still exists, for poor dark-skinned people in Jamaica. It was something he had kept locked up for years and there was clear guilt that he, as a Jamaican icon, had never talked about how Jamaica still needed to deal with its colonial past. But the story that a younger generation didn't know was how pivotal he had been in inspiring an earlier generation of black people. The great black history lesson was about him and that fantastic West Indies victory of 1976. Most of the young people listening to his outpourings on decolonising the curriculum had no idea that Michael Holding was probably the greatest fast bowler on the planet. The real question then is: how did he become so great?

OWZAT!

In 1976, I was 17 and doing my A levels at South London College (formerly West Norwood College). A strange place, it was characterised by a clear racial divide between the black students, most of whom were doing vocational courses or repeating their O levels, and those from white and other ethnic groups who were studying for A levels. The division was even more stark in the social area, which extended into the cafeteria. Young black men seemed to spend all their time playing snooker, listening to music and missing their classes. Lambeth Council soon got wind that they were subsidising aspiring snooker champions who didn't even live in the borough – and, unfortunately, few black kids ever became snooker professionals. The college was sold off and became a bus garage and storage facility.

For black Londoners, the harsh years of the 1970s were eased not only by Jamaican reggae but also by the soothing voice of radio presenter Alex Pascall. He was our universal uncle, whose groundbreaking show *Black Londoners* ran for over 14 years. Pascall came from Grenada, and he fought hard back in 1974 to get his show on the air. It was a magazine programme that featured some great celebrity interviews with the likes of Muhammad Ali, Bob Marley and an array of black political figures. By 1978, the BBC had given him a daily slot and he had serious coverage, with 60% of black Londoners tuning in to the show.

Speaking to *The Guardian* in September 2020, he recalled the reality of being black in the 1970s:

'I was nearly killed on the Holloway bridge.' His face tightens. 'I was coming out from a club and as I walked towards the bridge, I heard voices from both sides saying, "N—r, N—r, N—r! Get him, get him!" They were closing in on me. But as they got closer, a black cab turned up, the door was pitched open, and all I heard from the driver was: "Jump, darkie!" I leapt in, and the teddy boys were hanging on to the door, but he managed to drive off. And when we got to the beginning of …' Pascall falls silent, takes a sharp breath, and puts his hands to his eyes as they start to water. For a full 20 seconds he remains silent.

When he eventually starts to speak again, I ask what he was thinking of. 'Death,' he says. And after another long pause, adds: 'It's tough.'[2]

Given this real experience of nearly being killed because he was black, you knew that Uncle Alex would not hold back when it came to sharing the black experience. I loved his ability to convey our pain and our joy. What he also understood was that we needed hope. The madness of the 1970s was going to stay in the psyche for a long time after, and we needed an outlet to share the stories, to protest – and also to know that success was possible. He was on his best form during 1976, the year of the West Indies cricket tour of England.

Cricket had always been a big feature of my life, owing to my father's influence. I was never any good at it but, for my father, the game was almost a religion. He was devoted to his beloved West Indies cricket team, to the extent that its success had an impact on how he felt about living in Britain and his romantic desire to return home. This passion started out healthily enough but ultimately played a part in his mental collapse and demise. One of the problems facing all immigrants is thinking about 'back home'. The past becomes sentimentalised, and the present feels like a tough journey – rather like Odysseus hoping to return to the ideal of Ithaca. There is an awful cognitive dissonance in escaping a place that offered few opportunities and yet feeling great affection and nostalgia for it. My father defended his homeland as if it were a paradise.

During the 1975–76 season, the West Indies team was thrashed 5–1 in Australia, where it proved unable to cope with the home side's fast bowlers like Jeff Thomson and Dennis Lillee. I heard little about this defeat on the Caribbean grapevine – which tended to censor the bad news. However, there was great anticipation about the imminent summer tour of England, with five Tests to come. For my father and his Caribbean peers, this was war. It was so much more than just cricket: racism was still persistent, particularly with the police and employment, and my father needed a symbolic sense of victory. What made this Test series even more combative were some comments made by the England captain, Tony Greig. The cricket writer Simon Lister recalls how the Test series came to revolve around his use of the word 'grovel':

> Greig was the captain of England, but he wasn't *from* England. No, he was from South Africa. When Greig was a boy, he played cricket in his back garden in a nice part of Queenstown in the Eastern Cape, where a black domestic help and gardener called Tackies – conveniently named after the plimsolls he wore – bowled to him. Greig was good and came to England to play county cricket for Sussex. Within a decade he was captain of his adopted country and one day found himself sitting on the pavilion roof at Hove, speaking to the BBC. It was two days before the first Test of 1976.
>
> 'I think you must remember that the West Indians, these guys, if they get on top, they are magnificent cricketers, but if they're down, they grovel. And I intend, with the help of Closey and a few others, to make them grovel.'[3]

What we didn't realise then was that the West Indies team had to accomplish a radical transformation to stand a serious chance on the England tour. In response to the drubbing at the hands of Australia, captain Clive Lloyd had transformed the side with a new focus on fast bowling. The team now had lots of flair and style but Lloyd knew that even this was not enough. What else was needed? Simon Lister quotes Lloyd's words:

> The first thing you must do is create the right mind-set in the players and instil the right values. You then have to emphasise the importance of fitness, physical skills, especially

mastery of the basic skills, as well as mental skills like clear thinking, concentration, self-discipline, handling pressure, dealing with different game situations and continuous learning. I believe that those values and the sense of family contributed greatly to the closeness of the team and to its outstanding success.[4]

Culturally, the Caribbean is a diverse space – and this diversity plays out at the crease. Jamaicans tend to be aggressively on the front foot, Barbadians more reserved, waiting to hit the right ball, and the Latin Trinidadians will swing uninhibitedly at any loose ball. Of course, these are stereotypes, but it holds that each island has its own flavour of play. The Clive Lloyd era maintained a balance of these flavours, even while his leadership achieved the perfect combination of the managerial and the inspirational. In the backroom he was dealing with huge egos and big cultural differences – he had to fuse a disparate group of cultures and personalities into one unit. On the pitch, he led by example. He was a great batsman and a natural leader.

Clive Lloyd didn't look like the traditional idea of a sportsman. In fact, he looked more like a university professor, his large glasses and large moustache giving him the air of a deep thinker. Good leaders play two important roles. On the one hand they make sure that things get done, that the team has the knowledge, training, skills and discipline to execute their tasks. But at the same time there needs to be vision. In 1976, Lloyd seemed to understand that this was about more than cricket. It was about achieving victory over the old colonial masters and – for us – over the persistent racism that we faced in Britain. I have seen documentaries in which West Indies players claimed they were inspired to go the extra mile because of the 'grovel' comments by Tony Greig, and no doubt this was a factor. But there is a danger in giving this too much credit, as we paint a picture of a David and Goliath contest. Ultimately, the West Indies won because they were the better side.

I can't remember any day when my father's generation felt so proud. Everyone seemed to walk around as if they were kings and queens. They would dine out on 1976 for decades. My father was proud of his team but, like West Indies cricket, he would suffer a decline from which he would never recover. He died of lung cancer at the early age of 59, unable to return to his promised land of Jamaica. I knew how inspired he was by players like Michael Holding. But the players were not on a political mission – they wouldn't have indulged in bending the knee. For us, their strength came from their distance; they represented a space free from white British racism. They were gods who could inspire. In an interview from 2020 Holding says:

> I remember the summer of 1976 in England when letters would come to the dressing room for us [West Indies] play-ers, with racist messages: 'Go back home, crawl back to the trees,' and such. We as a team decided to ignore them, and I personally could do that easily because I knew I was going back home after the tour. But it also made me understand and appreciate why the West Indies cricket team's performance mattered so much to black people in the UK. They could walk with their heads held high to their workplaces next morning. They could look into the eyes of their colleagues and feel, 'I know I am as good as you.'[5]

There is so much to learn here about the nature of success. Only months earlier, the West Indies had been destroyed by Australia; the captain understood that he had to reframe what it meant to be a West Indian cricketer. No longer was he the happy-go-lucky calypso singer who flashed at every delivery. He was a cricketing professional, who understood that you took each ball on its merits.

In 2011 the Guyanese journalist Rudi Webster took time to remember the glorious summer of 1976. His analysis locates Clive Lloyd as an Odysseus figure, with an emphasis on vision and strategy. He reflects on his interview with Lloyd after the Australian disaster and how he set out to completely revolutionise the team:

> Clive had a lot of ability and skill in his side, but he knew that talent alone would not be enough to transform his side into a champion team. He would need other things in his change package: a clear vision, strategic thinking, good preparation, first-class leadership, great teamwork, good motivation, strong self-discipline, good mental control and high standards of execution on the field.
>
> Good leaders usually build their leadership on two strong pillars. They create an agenda for change in which they articulate their vision for the team, and design an intelligent strategy to achieve that vision. Then, they put together a unified and highly motivated network of people to implement that agenda. Clive followed that blueprint.
>
> He talked to me about his agenda for change over a few drinks in a Melbourne pub in 1976 soon after our disappointing Test series against Australia. He showed me his vision of what he wanted his team to achieve and

become – the best team in the world for the next 10 years – and he explained his strategic plan for realising that vision. He then told me that he would search the Caribbean for players with the right stuff and would turn them into a highly motivated and disciplined group, committed to implementing that agenda.[6]

It was Lloyd's use of four fast bowlers that really changed the craft of West Indies cricket. These bowlers were like dancers: they looked beautiful as they went through their ritualised run-up with speed and grace. What Lloyd wanted was energy, enthusiasm, guile, hard work and discipline. I noticed that when he changed bowlers there would be respect for his decision. What emerged from the team was self-discipline and professionalism.

It is this that I would have liked to hear from Michael Holding: 1976 as a masterclass in success, not more identity trauma. I wanted to hear the story of how a team came up in the world; of how organised, professional and scientific black people really are. It is a world away from stereotypes around instinctive athleticism.

That's why I wrote this book. As I come to the end of it, I can't help but reflect on the spirit of 1976, and how it epitomises everything that I think we need to highlight about black success.

But 1976 is also personal to me. It is a link to my father, and I can't help but think there is something in that summer that has led me to where I am now: Jamaica, much like the returnees we met in the last chapter.

ALL THAT GREEK MANURE

The Odyssey is Homer's epic tale of Odysseus's ten-year struggle to return home after the Trojan War. While Odysseus battles mythical creatures and faces the wrath of the gods, his wife Penelope and his son Telemachus stave off suitors vying for Penelope's hand and Ithaca's throne. This is *the* great adventure story. It's the story of how a soldier, weary from a long war, is desperate to get home to his motherland, to his farm and crops. This is the Greek country king who wants to return to his plough. It seems fitting to end our story by looking at how I navigated my own journey back to a homeland, both literally and psychologically.

Like many of the post-war generation, my parents' decision to emigrate from Jamaica to the UK was driven by their great sense of adventure. My father, though, never truly settled in Britain and yearned for his homeland of Oracabessa, on the north-east coast of Jamaica. He was raised down the road from where Ian Fleming wrote the James Bond novels, and where Fleming had a private bay called Goldeneye. My father never returned to Jamaica. However, good fortune means I have been able to take his place there.

When my mother died, I decided to use my part of the inheritance to buy my own apartment overlooking the Caribbean, not far from where my father grew up. Like Odysseus, I had returned home – in my case, driven by my father's spirit. This was not some sentimental or romantic or hedonistic decision to sit on the beach. I had plans to transform the local area. I saw my share of the family legacy as an opportunity to fulfil the story of the Parable of the Talents, perhaps the Bible at its most capitalist. I love the story in the

Revised English Version, the version that used to be left in hotel rooms:

For it will be as when a man going on a journey called his servants and entrusted to them his property; to one he gave five talents, to another two, to another one, to each according to his ability. Then he went away.

He who had received the five talents went at once and traded with them; and he made five talents more. So also, he who had the two talents made two more talents. But he who had received the one talent went and dug in the ground and hid his master's money.

Now, after a long time the master of those servants came and settled accounts with them. And he who had received the five talents came forward, bringing five talents more, saying, 'Master, you delivered to me five talents; here I have made five talents more.'

His master said to him, 'Well done, good and faithful servant; you have been faithful over a little, I will set you over much; enter into the joy of your master.'

And he who had the two talents also came forward, saying, 'Master, you delivered to me two talents; here I have made two talents more.'

His master said to him, 'Well done, good and faithful servant; you have been faithful over a little, I will set you over much; enter into the joy of your master.'

He also who had received the one talent came forward, saying, 'Master, I knew you to be a hard man, reaping where you did not sow, and gathering where you did not winnow; so, I was afraid, and I went and hid your talent in the ground. Here you have what is yours.'

But his master answered him, 'You wicked and slothful servant! You knew that I reap where I have not sowed, and gather where I have not winnowed? Then you ought to have invested my money with the bankers, and at my coming I should have received what was my own with interest.

'So, take the talent from him, and give it to him who has the ten talents. For to everyone who has will more be given, and he will have abundance; but from him who has not, even what he has will be taken away.'

—Matthew 25:14–30

I love these Judaeo-Christian stories. They strip you back to the very issue of your humanity. What have *you* done with *your* talents? Since I have spent most of my life in talent development, this parable was always my number-one story. We must surely invest in our own talents. For me, I wasn't only going to invest my share of the family legacy, I was going to take high risks. I would buy a farm, not knowing anything about farming, in a remote part of Jamaica.

Homer's *Odyssey* is the story of coming home, of how to fight off the monsters and demons so you can happily find yourself back on your own land. I wanted to literally dig myself into the community of Jamaica, so I decided to look for a house with a farm. One of the sad things about rural Jamaica is the large swathes of scrubland, overgrown and unused for either farming or housing. I was lucky to find a piece of it in Oracabessa: seven acres of overgrown farmland with a half-built house. The property had been owned by a Jamaican who had worked in America. He came home to build his five-bedroom mansion but, at the age of 91 and with failing health, had to sell and move to a smaller apartment building nearby. In a way, our stories were parallels: he had fulfilled his dream by returning to his childhood home, just as my father had not.

I decided, in my usual pragmatic way, to make his dream work. I would finish his house, develop the farm and revitalise the local community. As I write, we are in the middle of the project and the plan is to make the house and farm into a cultural wellness centre – a place that people can visit when they are tired of just sitting on the beach. They will be able to walk, talk and learn about the local produce; they will be able to pick what they want, and come up to the house for a meal produced from the farm. Each month Oracabessa High School will perform scenes from a Shakespeare play produced in a Jamaican context. 'Sewellness Park' seems the right name for this business. My parents will be able to rest, as I proudly wear the crown that has been paid for by my ancestors.

The great St Lucian poet Derek Walcott never bought into the despair of those who see the Caribbean as a colonial back-water badly in need of reparations. Rather, he saw it as a farm that needs to be cultivated and shaped. The tools for this job are not going to be some kind of anti-colonial rhetoric about dead white men and the historic burden of slavery. Walcott could see the potential in what has been left post-colony. He, like me, was tired of the same old voices that comment about the Caribbean. He wrote: 'in the New World, servitude to the muse of history has produced a literature of recrimination and despair, a literature of revenge written by the descendants of slaves, or a literature of remorse written by the descendants of masters.'[7]

This white-guilt literature hangs like a weight on me every time I go back to Britain: these people never see the region as having its own agency. Once again, it's about *them* and how in the end *they* can have power over others. In this way, the guilty white liberal becomes guilty of a new kind of colonialism. Like Walcott, I see a people who were *not* broken by slavery. A people able to shape their own history and their own future. This doesn't justify the horror of slavery and the centuries of racism. But, as farmers, we plant again – this time using all that was left behind to fertilise a new beginning.

Walcott wrote in his Nobel Acceptance Speech:

Break a vase and the love that reassembles the fragments is stronger than that love which took its symmetry for granted when it was whole. The glue that fits the pieces is the sealing of its original shape. It is such a love that reassembles our African and Asiatic fragments, the cracked heirlooms whose restoration shows its white scars. This gathering of broken pieces is the care and pain of the Antilles, and if the pieces are disparate, ill-fitting, they contain more pain than their original sculpture, those icons and sacred vessels taken for granted in their ancestral places. Antillean art is this restoration of our shattered histories, our shards of vocabulary, our archipelago becoming a synonym for pieces broken off from the original continent. And this is the exact process of the making of poetry, or what should be called not its 'making' but its remaking, the fragmented memory.[8]

That's exactly what we are doing at Sewellness Park: we are putting the fragments of memory back together again. I will proudly work with Oracabessa High School to put on great Shakespeare plays, set in a Jamaican context and resonating with Jamaican language and rhythm. Why? Because that's how we make the fragments cohere. That's how a great farmer looks at the land and uses the seeds to produce more growth – or as Walcott says in his poem *Omeros*: 'All that Greek manure under the green bananas'. Those great Greek stories are good shit, able to revitalise and fertilise Caribbean imagination and agency.

None of this would have been possible if Caribbeans had not also found success in Britain. Like Odysseus, we have won the war in Troy. Britain has changed significantly. Yes, it still has real problems of racism; it would be naive to deny it. However, I started to build my farm at the same time that Britain got its first ethnic minority prime minister. What struck me most was the fact that no one seemed to think twice about this monumental and historic shift.

SIREN SONG

The opening lines of Homer's poem give us a clue about the new challenges that we face, after gaining freedom:

> Muse, sing for me about that versatile man,
> Who sacked the sacred city of Troy
> And then wandered far and wide.
>
> —*Odyssey* 1:1–2[9]

For me, the muse was my mother – constantly reminding me that racism was not a figment of my imagination, but that I had all the powers I needed to beat it. Once this monster was slain, I could better get on with my new adventure: the fight with the wider world. I would have to use my brainpower to succeed in this new arena. One challenge was: do I just do stuff for the sake of it, or do I move onward with some purpose? I realised that my parents came to Britain mostly for the adventure, but that they quickly became pragmatists (e.g. by joining informal saving schemes and buying their own house). Did I have the potential, material and otherwise, for something more?

My favourite story in *The Odyssey* is the one about the Sirens. Odysseus decided that the way to get through the straits where the song of the Sirens seduced mortals like himself to their deaths was to listen to the beautiful music – but safely. He gave his men the wonderful technology of earplugs made out of wax; but decided to ignore this easy option for himself. Instead, he strapped himself to the mast and allowed the Sirens to do some intense wooing, knowing that he would never be pulled away from the security of his boat. The big question is why he didn't just use the same earplugs as his men: why put himself through all the trouble and the risk? The answer is that he wanted to test his courage against the gods. The challenge of the Sirens was indeed a treacherous one. But it can be seen as a sort of training session, in which Odysseus is testing the capacity of body and mind.

Those with courage will always need to withstand the Siren songs of false security. For black people, one form of false security is offered by what the US anthropologist Signithia Fordham calls 'fictive kinship'. Speaking of African-American culture, she says:

> Thus, the hypothesised fictive kinship system is African-Americans' premier prestige system in their imagined nation-state, conveying the idea of brotherhood and sisterhood of all African-Americans, regardless of class, gender, or sexual orientation. A sense of peoplehood or collective social identity

exists within the group. This collective, appropriated identity is evident in the various kinship terms that Black Americans use to refer to one another, such as 'brother,' 'sister,' and 'blood.'[10]

For Fordham, this imagined black unity is unstable, contradictory, and expresses itself in different ways throughout history. She says that it persists alongside racism in America.

Conversely, Odysseus is a lone hero. There is a sense that he is not bound to any collective identity. The crucial thing for his success is his agency and resourcefulness. The unity Fordham talks about can sometimes be a Siren song. It's tempting, beautiful and beguiling ... but it can also cause us to crash our ships against the rocks. When our fellows tell us that to do well in school is 'to act white', then the collective becomes a barrier to our own achievement. It's at this point that we need some sturdy earplugs, not to mention the courage to go against a counterproductive mindset.

I see this dynamic in the UK all the time. In my own book *Black Masculinities and Schooling* I charted the struggle of high-achieving black students with an anti-school subculture. Those who succeeded had navigation skills straight out of the Odysseus playbook. They were cunning enough to give some red meat to their peers while still being able to please their teachers. Like Odysseus, they would engage with the Sirens, listen to their beautiful song, while keeping themselves strapped down to the mast. Often, the straps that held firm were strong family backgrounds, reinforced by religious or ritualistic cultures in which elders are revered.

Sadly, even those with strong, stable backgrounds sometimes loosen their straps and are beguiled by the Sirens. As an example of this I will cite a friend of mine, a man of

African-Caribbean background who has two daughters studying medicine at top universities: one at Cambridge, the other
at University College London. The girls had attended a local
state school, were loving their time at university, and were, in
a sense both academic and personal, a success. However, many
of this man's friends had children who were either excluded
from school or underachieving. My friend felt that he couldn't
celebrate his daughters' success, and in fact told the one at
Cambridge not to say anything to the wider community. He
told me he didn't want to rub his success into others' faces. This
idea that you betray your community when you succeed in the
mainstream is a trap we need to avoid. Those girls deserve a
party every weekend: they should be held up as exemplars, and
this should be shared with all the community. Like Odysseus,
my friend needed the courage to break from those 'fictive kinship' obligations. He should be proud that he and his daughters
have done well in mainstream society. They are not only happy
individuals, but they also have life-saving skills.

In an interview in *Esquire* magazine, Idris Elba spoke
directly about how he does not define himself as a 'black actor'
because he sees the skill of acting as transcending the category
of race. He explained how he saw racism as 'very real', but 'only
as powerful as you allow it to be'. He thinks we 'are obsessed
with race' and 'that obsession can really hinder people's aspirations, hinder people's growth'.[11] With all this, I agree.

There was, however, a heavy backlash on social media, with
Elba being accused of betrayal and naivety. Like me, he has
acknowledged the reality of racism, but knows that his skill
has been the real determining factor of his success. What he
also acknowledges is that crossing the barriers of nation, class,
locality and accent has meant that he is considered for multiple

roles. He came onto the scene playing an African-American in *The Wire* – and nobody seemed to know that he grew up in Canning Town, East London. He has been part of a wave of black British actors who have stormed Hollywood, getting leading roles because of their classical training.

This is how Elba explains his motivation:

> I didn't become an actor because I didn't see black people doing it and I wanted to change that. I did it because I thought that's a great profession and I could do a good job at it. As you get up the ladder, you get asked what it's like to be the first black to do this or that. Well, it's the same as it would be if I were white. It's the first time for *me*. I don't want to be the first black. I'm the first Idris.

For me, the strongest words in his interview are when he says, 'I stopped describing myself as a black actor when I realised it put me in a box. We've got to grow. We've got to.'

How do we encourage this sort of growth? The place to start is employment. In the UK, America and Jamaica, there is a serious disparity when it comes to employment outcomes for young black people. Too many are either not working or doing dead-end jobs. If we are going to win big, then yes, acknowledge that we still have issues about race and colourism: that battle is not over. However, the bigger war this side of the twentieth century is skills and professions. Here the best start is an education that will give you the building blocks to become a professional, be it in the arts or sciences. The new winners, no matter what their background, will be those who have the tools to impact the world. We can take our inspiration from Odysseus, as described by the scholar Edith Hall:

The other Odyssean characteristic is implied by his epithet 'poutropos', one meaning of which is that he is 'able to turn his hand to many things' or 'versatile'... This is allied to another of his epithets, 'polumetis', 'capable of many kinds of cunning'. Odysseus has a plethora of skills; he is an all-rounder, an archetypal 'Renaissance man', who would in the twentieth century be as at home in a DIY store as at a university seminar or on a football pitch. He is a gifted carpenter, who builds a seagoing vessel in four days, from tree-felling to sail-making; he also fitted a whole bedroom for himself and Penelope. An expert navigator, he can steer his route by the stars. He is a confident peasant farmer, even as a child given by his father his own orchard and vineyard and who could beat Eurymachus in a ploughing race any time ... But these manual skills sit alongside his aristocratic training in athletics, he is a champion wrestler, discus-thrower, spear-thrower and boxer ... There is scarcely a manly pursuit for which he does not offer himself as an idealised forerunner. [12]

Odysseus inherited a vineyard from his father. Indirectly, I also inherited a Jamaican farm from my parents. This inheritance has been a learning experience: it made me realise how disconnected I was from the land. My Jamaican farm workers taught me the local names and benefits of a range of plants and herbs. I walked through fields of cerassie, a green bush plant that is simply boiled and drained. It has a bitter taste and locals claim it's good for most stomach ailments, including menstrual cramps. Another was aloe vera, or sinkle bible as the locals call it, which is a spiked green plant full of white cream great for constipation, high blood pressure, joint pains and so on. A third was fever grass, used for colds and as an anti-inflammatory.

Everywhere I walked, there was a plant or herb that had healing or health-beneficial properties.

As I walked my land, my local experts kept on about how the different herbs were good for constipation. The Jamaicans call this a 'wash out' – something that my mother told us was good for our system. So what is this obsession that Jamaicans have with shit?

I immediately turned to Freud for some psychoanalysis. Success in the Caribbean means many things, but expulsion of shit is a key priority. There's a link here to giving and taking. It's almost like it's a sin to hoard any surplus. It speaks to the need to be generous and give – outwards. Hence the good capitalist keeps their assets sufficiently 'liquid' to remain 'circulating': 'currency', after all, is what flows. As Jamaicans say, 'Money ah go run'. The message was clear to me that I had to make this farm profitable and give back to the local community. This was not because I was a do-gooder, but because it was healthy for my body and soul.

One of my key, ahem, outputs would be to upskill my community and apply high-level science to agriculture. The importance of skills education, particularly for the young, has been highlighted by the Jamaican academic Orlando Patterson. In his book *The Confounding Island,* he laments the collapse of the Jamaican education system, which continues to give poor results irrespective of good investment. He points to the best outcomes coming from out-of-school skills programmes:

The one successful element of the educational system is the HEART Trust/NTA (Human Employment and Resource Training Trust/National Training Agency), which provides vocational and technical training to unemployed and unattached youth in its own institutions, in on-the-job and community-based training at over a hundred centres. Not only should this program be expanded, but there should be greater integration and expansion of technical and vocational training within the formal primary and secondary sectors of the educational system.[13]

In a book with the subtitle *Jamaica and the Postcolonial Predicament*, he never once uses the word 'reparations'. This leading intellectual looks not only at the paradoxes of Jamaica's development but finds solutions in the practical agency of the people and policies that enhance it. He argues that local intelligence and vision can rebuild the island:

> The Canadian rural sociologist Tony Weis has proposed that 'historic possibilities could be opening for Jamaica's peasants' and for efficient small and mid-sized farmers, since the collapse of the island's plantation system may open up these lands to them. With an imaginative land reform program, Weiss speculates, 'lies the potential for a more economically viable, socially equitable, and ecologically rational agricultural landscape, dignified labour absorption and enhanced food security'.[14]

The smartest decision I made was to set up Generating Genius as a talent development programme in the key areas of Science, Technology, Engineering and Maths at a time when few people thought this was relevant to black communities. I knew the future would be about skills and the application of knowledge. There were still too few black people going into this key area;

far too much talent was being sucked into the public sector, which traditionally had been safe ground for black people. I wanted us to undergo that Odyssean test of self against the elements and the Siren voices, strapped to the mast of skills and knowledge in Science and Technology.

One of the themes of the *Odyssey* is exile. The idea of being cut off from an African ancestry resonates powerfully in the Caribbean consciousness. For many Caribbeans, history is simply a curse; it has left us abandoned and shipwrecked – and the only lifeboat is the good ship 'White Reparations'. There is a prevailing sense that we need to reconnect, and that those involved in cutting us off need to pay for their past sins.

But what if we have made our own reparation, in terms of language, culture and music? What if we have created a new raft for ourselves after the shipwreck of slavery? I recognise the pain of Caribbean history but also see exile as an opportunity – one that may lead to a true homecoming after a huge battle with the ravages of a brutal history. What we have become is a fusion of Africa and Europe.

It is either visionless or downright dishonest to present this as some kind of defence of slavery. Those of us who have been exiled now dance to what the late Rex Nettleford would call an 'African rhythm, European melody'. When the poet Walcott writes of 'Greek manure under the green bananas', he's not justifying slavery. Quite the reverse: he's saying that we did get 'shat on', but that we were smart enough to use it as fertiliser for the imagination.

CONCLUSION: A GOOD STORY

When the Report of the Commission on Race and Ethnic Disparities was published, it was met by a wave of hostility. Walking out of my local Costa in Croydon, I met a black actress who I hadn't seen for about 15 years. Shopping trolley in hand, she had no interest in reminiscing about the good old days. Instead, she bluntly asked me why I had said that racism doesn't exist. My first reply was that I had never said anything of the sort in my life. I told her that some people in the media didn't want her to hear the whole story. Then I asked her if she had read the report. She said no. However, she didn't understand why anyone would want to say that our findings were wrong if this were not the case.

It's a pity that she, and many others, never saw the very many progressive recommendations in the Report, recommendations that would soon be implemented by the government. One of the most radical, and one that I'm truly proud of, was the proposal that police should use diversion programmes for young people instead of charging them for possession of class B drugs. Hundreds of black youths will now avoid a criminal record.

Around that time, corporations and liberal individuals alike seemed caught in the headlights of the protests surrounding George Floyd's murder. You could see that they wanted to do something, but they didn't know what. In Kafka's novel *The Trial*, the hero, K, is accused of an unspecified crime and spends the whole book trying to prove he is innocent. This sums up the dilemma of white liberal 'allies'. They were trying to say they weren't guilty, but they weren't entirely sure what it was they weren't guilty of.

To me, it looked and felt bizarre – everyone putting up black screens on social media and saying how sorry they were for being institutionally racist. But, during this moment of introspection, it seemed that no one wanted to look at the multiple causes of racial disparity. Nobody seemed to care that Britain had stripped away opportunities from its white and black working class. Nobody wanted to crunch the numbers on how some ethnic minorities had improved significantly, while others had been left behind. It was too complex a story, apparently. Instead, we were fobbed off with virtue signalling while the power base in charities, the BBC and the Labour Party remained unaltered. There was a lot of noise, but nothing changed. My mother would have called this 'crocodile tears'.

It was the then equalities minister, Kemi Badenoch, who crafted the excellent government response to our report *Inclusive Britain*. This has got to be the must-read for everybody who wants to see a framework for a better, fairer Britain. In her foreword she writes:

> *Inclusive Britain* sets out a raft of measures that translate the findings from the Commission's report into concrete action. In doing so, we've considered and responded to each of the report's 24 recommendations – in some cases going even further than the report envisaged. *Inclusive Britain* is a comprehensive plan that details 74 actions right across government, which together will put us on course towards a more inclusive and integrated society.

This was radical stuff, and I really felt that my Commission could walk tall, fully vindicated in the knowledge that we had got it right. How could anyone argue against wider representation in the recruitment of police, an office for health disparities, and diversion strategies for young people caught with class B drugs? These are just a few of a whole platform of radical recommendations, which were totally ignored by the critics because they perceived the Report to be regressive. The opposite was true: our Report meant that seriously radical and progressive measures on race disparity would now be government policy.

What was different is explained in the last section of Kemi's foreword:

> We do not agree with those who think that lack of opportunity should be seen solely through the prism of ethnic minority disadvantage. We do not believe that any group is less intrinsically capable than any other – ability is spread across the population. But opportunity is not.

She talks of creating opportunity in a way that is wider than just policies linked to race. It needs to be connected to other variables such as class, geography, family structure and individual motivation. What we get is a raft of race-disparity policies linked to the government's wider agenda of levelling up Britain. The implication is that this is a document for everyone, including the white working class. It will have specific measures to deal with racism, but it is smart enough to realise that all ethnic minorities are not the same and there are variables not linked to racism that drive race disparity. The introduction to *Inclusive Britain* says:

> The Commission also found that where persistent disparities between ethnic groups do exist, they are more likely to be

caused by factors other than racism and discrimination. Its analysis of the data revealed that there were greater differences between, and even within, different 'umbrella' ethnic groups, such as black and Asian, than compared to the white majority.

What works for ethnic minorities in poor areas will work for all groups. No one can claim special privilege. What works must work for everyone.

The surprising truth is that many of the race disparities were best unravelled not with affirmative action programmes but within a wider levelling-up policy. This is summed up in part of the preamble of *Inclusive Britain*:

> By focusing on the places with the poorest socio-economic outcomes, levelling up acts as a vehicle for improving outcomes for the groups with the worst outcomes, complementing and supporting our wider work to tackle race and ethnic disparities.

The idea that a rising tide lifts all boats is a powerful one. But in terms of crafting policies, you have to understand that some of those boats have holes in them, they are in need of more specific intervention. It's for precisely this reason that there are 74 action plans, to ensure we get opportunity for all without sinking into a sea of division.

One of the best commentaries on my Report came from the theologian John Root, who used it to talk about the tension between 'good story' and 'bad story'. By this he means the 'perspectival diversity' whereby people can tell a story about the same situation (race in Britain) and come out with quite different narratives. He applauds our Report for avoiding 'optimism bias' by acknowledging a persistent wrong (racism) – but at the same time emphasising the real progress made. It's a complex balance that doesn't dismiss 'lived experiences', which are often negative, but at the same time acknowledges the 'good story' in the objective data. Fundamentally, it extols human agency. Root says:

> An appropriate starting point is the controversial Sewell Report of 'The Commission on Racial and Ethnic Disparities', which chose – against the mainstream academic perception of race in Britain – to tell a 'good story'. Racism, the Commission argues, whilst unquestionably real, was by no means the only source of racial and ethnic disparities; rather Sewell also fore-grounded social class, differences between ethnic groups and cultures, or British regions, as also being significant factors. Disparities, then, could not be unequivocally laid at the door of racism, including undefined and carelessly applied expla-nations focussing on systemic or institutional racism. Rather Sewell chose to produce considerable statistical evidence of other factors underlying racial disparities. As regards 'race', overall and certainly against the widely held consensus, we had a 'good story' to tell rather than a 'bad story'.[15]

He goes on to spell out the destructive effects of only indulg-ing the 'bad story'. This feeds a new kind of racism that leaves black populations as sad, powerless victims, stuck in a narrative of despair:

> For in reality, overall, a good story has been in the ascendant. Emphasising this has heuristic value, that is it provides a more positive way of seeing the world; it helps build up momentum

to seek an even better, more just world. It is antidote to a helpless and hopeless sense of passivity, and to the atrophying of a sense of agency. My sense is that this motivation lay in part behind the Sewell Commission's intention to emphasise the 'good story'.

That has been the point of this book. I do not wish to prosecute old arguments, but rather to tell the 'good story'. I want to shout about black success wherever I see it, and I want to encourage people to think about how they can go and get it. For that reason, courage and a sense of adventure are the qualities linking my key players. Mary Seacole was closer to a Greek hero than a caricature of black nationalism. She says in her autobiography: 'Some people ... have called me quite a female Ulysses. I believe that they intended it as a compliment.' She was no team player: hers was an individual's drive against her own limits with Odysseus as role model. Similarly, the Learning Trust in Hackney showed courage in insisting on the best model for black achievement: school leaders focussed on high standards and high expectations. And we had the sense of adventure to take a group of young black boys to a place, educationally, where they had never been before.

At Generating Genius, we had to be brave. Luckily, I had the backing of a corporate sector desperate for STEM talent. They not only funded the programme but gave our students great careers. This was not down to some kind of race allocation: it was because they needed talent, and we could give it to them. We provided a fantastic ladder for these low-income black students, providing guidance throughout their career development from ages 12 to 24. I don't remember once mentioning the word 'black' to them. Was this because we were ashamed of our cultural background? Was I trying to ignore the realities of racism? Of course not. I needed to draw their focus to quantum mechanics, calculus and the intricacies of coding in Python.

Our students were aware of the reality of race and racism. I didn't need to teach them that. On the other hand, they didn't have a clue about data science.

We had to take on all the risks of running a charity, as we exposed our students to a fantastic education. At every stage there was a real danger that the whole programme would collapse: what if there was no interest, what if there was no funding? I never worried. I knew I would be able to realise my vision because the project was based on a simple reality: if we gave these kids a shot, they'd shoot.

So many have loved our coding courses. They are now flying high in large tech companies. It's for that reason I feel some concern that the burgeoning 'diversity and inclusion' sector, valued at around five billion pounds, is sucking up black talent. Students who should be going into the mainstream of a business, looking to get to the top armed with tech skills, are instead helping companies figure out how to diversify. I don't dismiss the need for this kind of work: companies need to look at the range of talent that they bring to their industries. But we can have all the hiring schemes in the world, yet if young black people – or indeed young people generally – enter the workplace without technical skills, they're going to struggle. To address this wider issue will take courage, risk-taking and a strategy that can turn big ideas into programmes that deliver.

FINAL THOUGHTS

A friend of mine asked me why I wanted to go into farming. As a successful academic, and now parliamentarian, why would I want to get mixed up in the grubby business of tilling the land? I must admit, outside of Jamaica I know few farmers who look like me. That is all the evidence I need to know that I'm doing the right thing. I don't want to be involved in anything prescribed to me by what's expected. Farming in Jamaica, I've never felt so free from white guilt and expectations. Nobody can come and tell me how I ought to be. Nobody can assert power over me. Nobody will cause me to ignore the hard reality of the Parable of the Talents. My farm will soon make money, and I will employ lots of local people to help me. Why? Because I'm going to force it to make money, and as soon as it does, I'm going to plough that money into employing others. It's me who is doing that – not some invisible wind or hidden force. It's personal agency.

This story, this *good* story, begins and ends with the powerful idea of agency. It's inside all of us. No matter how many obstacles are placed in our way, no matter if we get blown off course, if we use our courage, guile and, yes, our agency, we will continue the great tradition of black success.

APPENDIX

A SUMMARY OF THE RECOMMENDATIONS OF THE COMMISSION FOR RACE AND ETHNIC DISPARITIES

O N reflection, the Boris Johnson government of 2019–22 will be known for many things, including Brexit and the roll-out of the Covid vaccine. However, it may be the implementation of all 24 recommendations in my Report that comes to be seen as its most sustained achievement. Not all, but too many people in the media wanted the Report to be part of some big race war, with institutional racism deniers on one side and those pushing the George Floyd legacy on the other. Although nowhere in the Report did we deny institutional racism, it is clear that some just wanted us to be the 'bad guys'. In fact, we found that the disparities we investigated were complex, with many not really based on racism. Where there were structural racial issues, we responded with 24 progressive recommendations, all of which have now been implemented – thereby transforming crime and policing, the health service, education and employment. For many, the following summary of our recommendations will come as a surprise; for me and my fellow commissioners, however, this aspect of our work was always a major success.

BUILD TRUST

RECOMMENDATION 1
Challenge racist and discriminatory actions

Fund the Equality and Human Rights Commission (EHRC) to use its compliance, enforcement and litigation enforcement powers to challenge policies or practices that either cause significant and unjust racial disadvantage, or arise from racial discrimination.

Separately, the government should consider the complex issue of online abuse as a public policy priority.

RECOMMENDATION 2
Review the Care Quality Commission's (CQC) inspection process

Review the CQC's approach to including disparities in the experiences, progression and disciplinary actions taken against ethnic minority staff in their inspections of healthcare providers.

RECOMMENDATION 3
Improve the transparency and use of artificial intelligence

Issue guidance that clarifies how to apply the Equality Act to algorithmic decision-making and require transparency for public sector bodies when such is applied to decision-making concerning individuals.

RECOMMENDATION 4
*Bridge divides and create partnerships
between the police and communities*

Develop a minimum standard framework for independently chaired community 'Safeguarding Trust' groups that scrutinise and problem-solve alongside policing, and independently inspect forces against this minimum standard.

RECOMMENDATION 5
*Improve training to provide police officers with
practical skills to interact with communities*

Develop a strategy to improve the efficacy and implementation of stop and search, and de-escalation training ensuring a consistent approach is taken by all police force areas.

PROMOTE FAIRNESS

RECOMMENDATION 6
*Replicate the factors of educational
success for all communities*

Invest in meaningful and substantial research to understand and replicate the underlying factors that drive success of high performing groups.

RECOMMENDATION 7
*Invest in proven interventions through
better targeted funding*

Systematically target disparities in education outcomes between disadvantaged pupils and their peers through funding, considering geographical variation, ethnicity, gender and socio-economic status.

RECOMMENDATION 8
Advance fairness in the workplace

Develop resources and evidence-based approaches of what works to advance fairness in the workplace, and which are readily available to employers.

RECOMMENDATION 9
Investigate what causes existing ethnic pay disparities

Require publication of a diagnosis and action plan for organisations who choose to publish ethnicity pay figures. These should set out the reasons why any disparities exist and what will be done to address them.

RECOMMENDATION 10
*Improve understanding of the ethnicity
pay gap in NHS England*

Undertake a strategic review of the causes of disparate pay across NHS England and spell out the measures that might meaningfully address any disparities.

RECOMMENDATION 11
Establish an Office for Health Disparities

Establish a new office to properly target health disparities in the UK, focussing on research, communications and expertise to reduce health inequalities across all groups.

RECOMMENDATION 12
Prevent harm, reduce crime and divert young people away from the criminal justice system

Develop an evidence-based pilot that diverts offences of low-level class B drug possession into public health services.

RECOMMENDATION 13
Build social and cultural capital – enrichment for all

Phase in an extended school day prioritising disadvantaged areas to provide pupils with the opportunity to engage in physical and cultural activities that enrich lives and build social and cultural capital.

RECOMMENDATION 14
Increase legitimacy and accountability of stop and search through body-worn video

Increased scrutiny of body-worn video footage of stop and search encounters, with senior officer involvement required in cases where interactions are of concern and need improvement.

CREATE AGENCY

RECOMMENDATION 15
*Empower pupils to make more informed
choices to fulfil their future potential*

Issue guidance to higher education institutions to help reduce
disparities in applications at an earlier stage and monitored
for effectiveness.

RECOMMENDATION 16
Open up access to apprenticeships

Create a targeted apprenticeships campaign to inform young
people facing discrimination or disadvantage of the full range
of career pathways open to them and encourage them to take
up apprenticeships in growth sectors.

RECOMMENDATION 17
Encourage innovation

Pilot a new enterprise programme to nurture talent and encourage innovation, targeted at aspiring entrepreneurs from under-
represented and low-income backgrounds across the UK.

RECOMMENDATION 18
Improve safety and support for children at risk

Develop a digital solution to signpost and refer children and
young people at risk of, or already experiencing criminal
exploitation, to local organisations who can provide support.

RECOMMENDATION 19
Undertake a 'support for families' review

Undertake a review to investigate and take action to address the underlying issues facing families. This Commission has identified this as a significant contributing factor to the experience of disparities.

ACHIEVE INCLUSIVITY

RECOMMENDATION 20
Making of modern Britain: teaching an inclusive curriculum

Produce high-quality teaching resources, through independent experts, to tell the multiple, nuanced stories of the contributions made by different groups that have made this country the one it is today.

RECOMMENDATION 21
Create police workforces that represent the communities they serve

Introduce a local residency requirement for recruitment to each police force area, with the College of Policing developing guidance to support implementation.

RECOMMENDATION 22
*Equip the police service to serve the
needs of their local communities*

Design and evaluate recruitment pilots that match candidates'
life skills with the needs of the communities they serve in their
local areas.

RECOMMENDATION 23
Use data in a responsible and informed way

Develop and publish a set of ethnicity data standards to
improve understanding and information gathering, reducing
the opportunity for misunderstanding and misuse.

RECOMMENDATION 24
Disaggregate the term 'BAME'

Stop using aggregated and unhelpful terms such as 'BAME',
to better focus on understanding disparities and outcomes for
specific ethnic groups.

https://www.gov.uk/government/publications/
the-report-of-the-commission-on-race-and-ethnic-disparities/
summary-of-recommendations

NOTES

1. Penge: The School of Hard Knocks

1 John L. Williams *C. L. R James: A Life Beyond the Boundaries* (London: Constable, 2022) p. 30.
2 C. L. R. James *Beyond a Boundary* (London: Hutchinson, 1963).
3 John McWhorter *Losing the Race: Self-sabotage in Black America* (New York: Perennial, 2001) p. 115.

2. Finding My Voice: Gargoyles and Spider Gods

1 Martha Warren Beckwith *Jamaica Anansi Stories* (1924): https://sacred-texts.com/afr/jas/index.htm
2 According to *The Guardian*, 'there was something of a Citizen Kane in McCalla – and he was certainly an enigma; a man who owned an outspoken newspaper, whose voice was rarely heard. He shunned media interviews, and was an elusive figure even to the people he employed.'
3 Pope's role is discussed in a *Times* article by Peter McKenzie (13 January 2004): 'The editor credited with leading *The Voice* through its glory years, 1988 to 1991, is Steve Pope. It was he who led the charge against the police, and in particular the Metropolitan Police Commissioner Sir Paul Condon. One famous issue declared "Condon, you're an Ass!" when the commissioner gave a speech in which he suggested that 80 percent of muggers in some parts of London were black.'

Pope himself recalls: 'There were so many issues back then and racism was easier to spot. The paper gave the community a voice to discuss things that they were being charged with. Second-generation blacks welcomed *The Voice*. It spoke in a language and a voice that they recognised as one of their own. We provoked debate among the black community and we got the police and the politicians on the back foot.' https://www.thetimes.co.uk/article/out-of-tune-why-nobodys-listening-to-the-voice-qdh39qx5qf2

4   *The Voice*, 14 August 1990. Of the beleaguered South African pastor Allan Boesak, Marcia writes: 'His wife has now left him and it is overwhelmingly apparent that he will find it hard to regain the trust and respect that he once enjoyed. How many people in prison now wish they hadn't succumbed to the temptation to commit crime? How many single mothers are now regretting the decision to have that one night of passion? How many families lie broken because one member could not resist sexual temptation when it came their way?'

5   For me, one aspect of Marcia's column was really intriguing. I thought going to church was about worshipping God. After reading some of her copy, I began to think that I had got it wrong all these years: the best place to pull was not the nightclub but the church. Under the snappy headline 'Praying for Mr Right', Marcia gives some real practical advice to the hordes of Christian women in search of the right man: 'Christian women greatly outnumber men, leading many to believe that the only way they'll get married is to pray constantly! Aside from praying, there are many things a Christian woman can do to meet and marry the man of her dreams without leaving her faith.'

6   Tariq Modood and Richard Berthoud *The Fourth National Survey of Ethnic Minorities: Ethnic Minorities in Britain Diversity and Disadvantage* (London: Policy Studies Institute, 1994). The survey shows the Caribbean community achieving some of the worst social outcomes of ethnic minorities throughout the 1980s and early 1990s. It concludes: 'For arrears and money worries, though, there was a different pattern of hardship. Once income and household characteristics have been taken into account, the various Asian minority groups were either similar to white households, or rather less likely than whites to report these kinds of hardship. In contrast, as indicated in the

straightforward tables in the previous sections, Caribbean households were much more likely to report arrears and money worries, as well as a shortage of durables. These findings are illustrated in Figure 5.8, which clearly shows how the Caribbeans were worse off on all three measures. They may not have been far behind white people in a simple measure of income, but there is consistent evidence of financial hardship among Caribbeans which requires more detailed investigation.'

7 *Jamaica Gleaner* letters page, 2 September 2022.

8 Marcia Dixon, blog post on *Woman Alive*, 9 February 2022: https://www.womanalive.co.uk/opinion/marcia-dixon-mbe-on-her-journey-from-student-and-part-time-writer-to-the-queens-honours-list/6064.article

3. Cutting the Gordian Knot: The Hackney Learning Trust

1 Onyekachi Wambu 'Class act worth flunking', *The Voice*, 12 March 1996.

2 'Transforming education in Hackney', The Learning Trust, July 2012: https://education.hackney.gov.uk/sites/default/files/document/10%20Years%20in%20Hackney.pdf

3 'Aiming high: Supporting the effective use of EMAG', Department of Education and Schools, April 2004, Ref: DfES/0283/2004

4 Leon Tikly, Audrey Osler and John Hill 'The ethnic minority achievement grant: a critical analysis', *Journal of Education Policy* 20(3): pp. 283–312, May 2005.

5 Farrukh Dhondy, 'Institutional racism', *Times Educational Supplement*, 19 February 1999.

This quote remains the best comment to date on how we have used this concept to avoid the complexities surrounding race disparities. What is disturbing is how academics, report chairs and journalists declare their allegiance without fully understanding the term. In many ways it is no different from the way a religion protects its sacred texts.

6 Gus John quoted in *The Voice*, August 1996.

7 'Transforming education in Hackney', as above.

4. Generating Genius:
Six Steps to Success

1 Jon Entine 'The DNA Olympics – Jamaicans win sprinting "genetic lottery" – and why we should all care', *Forbes*, 12 August 2012.

2 'Champs – the biggest deal in Jamaica', *World Athletics*, 8 April 2014. In the same article the sprinter Warren Weir described Champs as 'probably the most competitive junior championship in the world. And it's more about teams, about getting the most points to make your school the champion.' https://worldathletics.org/news/feature/boys-girls-champs-jamaica-zharnel-hughes-issa

3 'Kartel shows his colours', *Jamaican Observer*, 4 April 2014.

4 *World Athletics*, as above.

5 'Jamaica's Coaches', *Jamaica Gleaner*, 28 March 2019.

6 'Chinese parents are keen on a more Confucian education', *Economist*, 20 May 2021: https://www.economist.com/china/2021/05/20/chinese-parents-are-keen-on-a-more-confucian-education

7 *Kingston Gleaner*, 20 July 2005.

8 M. E. Lamb and C. Lewis 'The development and significance of father-child relationships in two-parent families', in M. E. Lamb (ed.) *The Role of the Father in Child Development* (Hoboken N.J.: Wiley, 2004).

9 'Let's hear it from the boys', *Jamaica Gleaner*, 16 August 2005.

10 BBC Radio 4 interview with Dotun Adebayo, 13 November 2013: https://www.youtube.com/watch?v=n9BmhNhyEKo

11 Paul Johnson 'We need to understand diversity better', *The Times*, 5 December 2022: https://www.thetimes.co.uk/article/we-need-to-understand-the-diversity-of-experience-across-ethnic-groups-l7vbgzv99

12 Signithia Fordham and John Ogbu 'Black students' school success: Coping with the burden of "acting White"', *Urban Review* 18(3) pp. 176–206, 1986.

5. Nigeria's Scrabble for Britain:
The Reverse Missionaries

1 The BBC covered the victory, and when Nigeria's president, Muhammadu Buhari, phoned to congratulate him, Jighere beamed proudly and said: 'It felt so warm to have him speak with me right then and there. It was a very, very important experience. He told me how proud he is of my accomplishment and how proud I have made the nation as a whole, not just the nation but Africa as a whole. And that it has really gone to prove that we are truly the giants of Africa.' https://www.bbc.co.uk/news/world-africa-34764670

2 Malcolm Gladwell *David and Goliath: Underdogs, Misfits and the Art of Battling Giants* (London: Allen Lane, 2013).

3 This has been shown in a number of research papers, for example G. Q. J. Campoy's 'The effect of word length in short-term memory: Is rehearsal necessary?', *Experimental Psychology* 61(5): 724–34, May 2008. A number of psychological studies (e.g. Baddeley et al 1975, Campoy 2011 and Lalbert et al 2011) have indicated that we tend to remember short words more easily than long words. Longer words tend to 'decay' more quickly and are harder to bring to mind when you need them – for example in a game of Scrabble.

4 Rosie Bell 'Nigeria: the country that loves to overachieve', *BBC Travel*, 25 January 2021: https://www.bbc.com/travel/article/20210124-nigeria-the-country-that-loves-to-overachieve

5 Gina Yashere *Cack-Handed: A Memoir* (London: HarperCollins, 2021).

6 Remi Adekoya 'Not all the facts fit the anti-colonialist narrative', 7 August 2020: https://unherd.com/2020/08/anti-colonialists-must-tell-the-truth-about-empire/

7 Figures from a research project called 'Being Built Together' led by Andrew Rogers at Roehampton University between 2011 and 2013: https://www.roehampton.ac.uk/globalassets/documents/humanities/being20built20togethersb203-7-13.pdf

8 2021 Census data on religion and ethnicity, published by the Office for National Statistics (ONS) in November 2022.

9 Rakib Ehsan 'The changing face of British Christianity: Ethnic minorities have renewed British churches', *The Critic*, 2 December 2022.

10 Richard Assheton 'Reframed by Black Lives Matter, African art is an £11bn global hit', *The Sunday Times*, 6 November 2022. That Black Lives Matter stimulated a wider interest in African art cannot be denied. However, curators like Tokini Peterside were already working in the field and capitalised on the new interest.

11 See *Daily Mail* feature on 8 June 2023 headlined 'East London's state school rival to Eton strikes again! Academy in one of city's most deprived boroughs breaks its own record to receive 89 Oxbridge offers – despite Covid disruption': https://www.dailymail.co.uk/femail/article-10639291/Brampton-Manor-state-school-Newham-gets-89-Oxbridge-offers.html

The article goes on: 'How do they do it? The school's motto is "Success through effort and determination". Good teaching, early starts, long days and "normalising" academic success. This enables the students to achieve and thrive despite the many challenges in the borough, which is one of the poorest in the UK. Speaking to the online magazine, *The Interview*, Olukoshi says, "I consider every challenge I have faced as an opportunity to excel rather than an obstacle to overcome." There is also this observation: 'Like all good leaders, Olukoshi shares the credit for success with others. When he was awarded an OBE for his services to education, he said, "Although the honour was given to me, it really is for all the staff that have worked tirelessly over the years to help make a difference to the lives of our young people."'

6. Nursing the Wrong Image: The Curious Journey of Mary Seacole

1 David Mills 'Bootleg Black Bart Simpson, the hip-hop T-shirt star', *Washington Post*, 28 June 1990: https://www.washingtonpost.com/archive/lifestyle/1990/06/28/bootleg-black-bart-simpson-the-hip-hop-t-shirt-star/11b3b65d-4033-41da-a5f7-e13ea56ce498/

2 Robert Dingwall 'Black history and the myth of Mary Seacole', *Social Science Space*, 23 October 2016: https://www.socialsciencespace.com/2016/10/black-history-myth-mary-seacole/

3 *Daily Gleaner*, 9 June 1881.

4 Dingwall 'Black History and the Myth of Mary Seacole', as above. See also the fascinating article written by Ziggi Alexander for *B:M* in 2023: https://www.blackhistorymonth.org.uk/article/section/real-stories/mary-seacole-my-inalienable-right-to-self-identify-2/
Alexander was one of the researchers who restored Seacole to the public consciousness in the 1980s. The article reflects on her role as a black icon and does discuss the issue of her class/colour status.

5 Dingwall 'Black History and the Myth of Mary Seacole', as above.

6 Jane Robinson *Mary Seacole: The Most Famous Black Woman of the Victorian Age* (New York: Carroll & Graf, 2004) p. 43.

7 Robinson *Mary Seacole*, as above p. 141.

8 See for example Alasdair Gennie 'BBC criticised for implying Florence Nightingale was racist on top children's show *Horrible Histories*', *Daily Mail*, 30 September 2014.

9 Louise Bennett *Jamaica Labrish*, ed. Rex Nettleford (Kingston: Sangster, 1966).

10 Orlando Patterson, *The Confounding Island: Jamaica and the Postcolonial Predicament* (Cambridge, Mass.: Harvard University Press, 2019) p. 268. Patterson points to Bob Marley as the key ambassador of this music and he remains a global and marketing icon. In 1999, his 1977 album *Exodus* was named by *TIME* magazine as the album of the century. London and the music producer Chris Blackwell were pivotal to this success, which was nurtured by the new Caribbean community in the UK.

11 Chris Blackwell with Paul Morley *The Islander: My Life in Music and Beyond* (London: Nine Eight Books, 2022) p. 71.

12 Blackwell *The Islander*, as above p. 71.

13 Mike Phillips and Trevor Phillips *Windrush: The Irresistible Rise of Multi-racial Britain* (London: HarperCollins, 1998) p. 316.

14 Phillips and Phillips *Windrush*, as above p. 346.

15 Phillips and Phillips *Windrush*, as above p. 347.

7. The Housing Lark: How a People Built Their Future

1 James Berry *Fractured Circles* (London: New Beacon Books, 1979).

James was a thorn in the side of many black activists. He really hated the confinement of black nationalism. He was acutely aware of racism but could see the stranglehold of the new identity politics. Britain also offered a new intellectual freedom that he couldn't find in rural Jamaica.

2 Berry *Fractured Circles*, as above.

3 Under the chairmanship of Sir E. Milner Holland, this was the most comprehensive modern survey of London housing and paid particular attention to the relations between occupiers of rented accommodation and private landlords. Its findings helped to inform the Race Relations Act of 1965, which banned open racial discrimination in housing.

4 Samuel Selvon *The Housing Lark* (London: Penguin Classics, 2020).

5 Mike Phillips and Trevor Phillips: *Windrush: The Irresistible Rise of Multi-racial Britain* (London: HarperCollins, 1998).

6 Z. Nia Reynolds *When I Came to England: An Oral History of Life in 1950s and 1960s Britain* (London: Black Stock Books, 2014).

7 Reynolds *When I Came to England*, as above.

8 Tariq Modood and Richard Berthoud *The Fourth National Survey of Ethnic Minorities: Ethnic Minorities in Britain, Diversity and Disadvantage* (London: Policy Studies Institute, 1994). The survey was undertaken in 1994 by the Policy Studies Institute and Social and Community Planning Research. A nationally representative sample of 5,196 people of Caribbean and Asian origin were interviewed in detail, together with a comparison sample of 2,867 white people.

9 Modood and Berthoud *The Fourth National Survey of Ethnic Minorities*, as above.

10 Nigel de Noronha 'Housing and the older ethnic minority population in England', Race Equality Foundation, February 2019: https://www.housinglin.org.uk/_assets/Resources/Housing/Support_materials/Briefings/HLIN_Briefing_BME_Housing.pdf

11 Eleanor Marie Brown 'Why Black homeowners are more likely to be Caribbean-American than African-American in New York: A theory of how early West Indian migrants broke racial cartels in housing', GWU Legal Studies Research Paper No. 2016-23, June 2016.

12 Heather Ayn Horst 'Back a yaad: Constructions of home among Jamaica's returned migrant community', doctoral thesis, University College London, 2004. In her abstract Horst writes:

'This thesis investigates return migration among Jamaicans who migrated to the United Kingdom after WWII and retired in Jamaica throughout the 1990s. Focusing upon the processes of rebuilding a life at "home", it examines the ways in which returning migrants utilise material culture to transgress the sense of alienation from land and people in Jamaica, and explores the relationship between particular objects of material culture and the politics of identity. Based upon 12 months of ethnographic fieldwork in a central Jamaican town, the study analyses transformations in returnees' sense of being English and/or Jamaican, from perceiving England as "the mother country" to the frustration and disillusionment felt after migration resulting in a more concrete sense of being black Jamaican immigrants living in England. Upon returning to postcolonial Jamaica, notions of being English and Jamaican are further questioned as returnees come to terms with local Jamaicans' categorisation of returnees as "English". Returnees seek to construct lifestyles which counteract the years of hard work endured to return and retire in Jamaica, the large houses and consumer goods both assert and assist in the creation of a lifestyle of leisure and enjoyment. Yet, local Jamaicans' constant requests for money and goods accompanied by media portrayals of crime produce feelings of vulnerability, resulting in a heightened use of security as well as an increased desire to reintegrate into Jamaican society particularly through patterns of exchange. In this context, funerals assume a prominent role, enabling returnees to literally and symbolically locate a sense of community and return. Funeral participation also aids in counteracting a sense of alienation from land and people by redefining "home" as a spiritual return to heaven, highlighting the dynamic nature of home as a concept and space for negotiating identity.'

13 Horst 'Back a yaad', as above.

8. Odysseus and the Five Talents: Reaping What You Sow

1 Michael Holding interviewed by Sriram Veera 'All people of colour who hit out at racism, their careers ended in no time', *Indian Express,*

29 June 2021: https://indianexpress.com/article/sorts/cricket/michael-holding-west-indies-cricket-racism-t20-7378608/

2 Joseph Harker, 'Alex Pascall: the broadcaster who gave a voice to black Britain – and is now taking on the BBC', *Guardian*, 3 September 2020: https://www.theguardian.com/society/2020/sep/03/alex-pascall-the-broadcaster-who-gave-a-voice-to-black-britain-and-is-now-taking-on-the-bbc

3 Simon Lister 'When death whispered: At the Oval in 1976, the bowler was Holding, the batsman was history', *Cricket Monthly*, January 2016: https://www.thecricketmonthly.com/story/953181/when-death-whispered

4 Lister 'When death whispered', as above.

5 Michael Holding interviewed by George Dobell 'What has English cricket been like for black players?', *Cricket Monthly*, June 2020: https://www.thecricketmonthly.com/story/1225596/what-has-english-cricket-been-like-for-black-players

6 Rudi Webster, 'Memories of Clive Lloyd's captaincy', *Kaieteur News*, 11 August 2011: https://www.kaieteurnewsonline.com/2011/08/07/memories-of-clive-lloyd%E2%80%99s-captaincy/

7 Derek Walcott, 'The Muse of History' in *What the Twilight Says* (London: Faber & Faber, 1998) p. 372.

8 Walcott *What the Twilight Says*, as above p. 48.

9 Homer *The Odyssey*, translated in Edith Hall *The Return of Ulysses: A Cultural History of Homer's Odyssey* (London: I. B. Tauris, 2008).

10 Signithia Fordham *Blacked Out: Dilemmas of Race, Identity and Success at Capital High* (Chicago, Ill.: University of Chicago Press, 1996) p. 72.

11 Idris Elba interviewed by Alex Bilmes 'Becoming Idris Elba', *Esquire*, 8 February 2023.

12 Edith Hall *The Return of Ulysses: A Cultural History of Homer's Odyssey* (London: I. B. Tauris, 2008) p. 102.

13 Orlando Patterson *The Confounding Island, Jamaica and the Postcolonial Predicament* (Cambridge, Mass.: Harvard University Press, 2019) p. 330.

14 Patterson *The Confounding Island*, as above p. 336.

15 John Root 'Good Story? Bad Story?', Substack No. 113, 28 March 2023: https://johnroot.substack.com/p/good-story-bad-story-lynnes-story